PREPARING
YOURSELF
for
GOD'S
PROMISES

PREPARING
YOURSELF
for
GOD'S
PROMISES

M. DENISE BACCUS

Bridge-Logos

Alachua, Florida 32615

Bridge-Logos
Alachua, FL 32615USA

Preparing Yourself for God's Promises
by M. Denise Baccus

Printed in the United States of America.

Library of Congress Catalog Card Number: 2008927489
International Standard Book Number 978-0-88270-476-0

Scripture quotations in this book are from the *King James Version* of the Bible.

Scripture quotations marked AMP are taken from *The Amplified Bible* edition identified as Copyright © 1984 by Zondervan Publishing House.

Scripture quotations marked TLB are taken from *The Living Bible*. ©1971. Used by permission of Tyndale House Publishers, Wheaton, Illinois 60189. All rights reserved.

Scripture quotations marked NIV are taken from the *Holy Bible, New International Version*®. NIV®. Copyright © 1973, 1978, 1984 by International Bible Society. Used by permission of Zondervan. All rights reserved.

G222.316.N.m806.35250

Dedication

**This book is dedicated to my children,
Jonathan and Cameron.**

Thank you for sharing me with the ministry.
I thank God every day that He chose me
to be your mother!

*Children are a blessing from God
and a lasting legacy.*

Acknowledgements

To my parents, James and Georgia Jackson: Thank you for rearing me in a godly home. I appreciate your love and support over the years. Thank you for letting me fail and succeed, and loving me through it all.

To Anointed Word Church: Thank you for providing a platform for me to teach the lesson that serves as the basis for this book.

To Elder Walrick Christie: Thank you for your prayerful support and motivating me to embrace my destiny.

To Professor Robert Thomson: Thank you for your mentorship and encouraging me in so many ways. All of the writing and research fostered much discipline and focus.

To the Church mothers of Morris Temple FBC: I will never forget your instruction and example of what it truly means to be a virtuous woman.

To my family: I Love You All!

CONTENTS

Preface

Have you ever wondered why some people seem "to have it all," while others lead a life littered with failed attempts to climb life's ladder of success? Well, the fact is that all of us were born with the potential for greatness. How can I be so sure? God created us to fulfill His purpose on the earth, to accomplish awesome things, and to share in His creative ability.

For example, if you ask a small child what he would like to do when he grows up, the response is usually highly ambitious. It is not unusual to hear "I want to build a jet or travel to the stars. I want to invent a flying car or find a cure for all diseases." However, somewhere between childhood and adulthood our expectations are often reduced to being an accountant, a secretary or a mechanic. Even though these are admirable professions, what happened to our dreams? The answer is that we began to limit ourselves by what our eyes beheld and what our ears heard.

However, I believe that God has recently caused your dreams to be reawakened. This book is simply a confirmation. I am absolutely convinced that there are no limits to your possibilities! God is yet "able to do exceeding abundantly above all that we ask or think, according to the power that worketh in us" (Ephesians 3:20).

This is not just another book written to explain why you have not yet received what God has promised you. On the contrary, I believe this book will explain just why you are at the critical point of receiving your grandest expectations. You have simply been in preparation for your expectation. Now that you are positioned for purpose, it is time for your godly vision to be realized.

I believe that as you read this book, you will be able to relate to each stage of preparation for your expectation. I literally *see* you checking off the heading of each chapter and saying "been there, done that." I firmly believe that as you are reading this book, God is going to confirm that you have been on the "right track" all along. For most of us, we are in the stage of restoration, wherein we are about to obtain all that we ever lost. But my friends, this is not the end of the blessing. The process is not complete until you experience the manifestation of your grandest expectation. May it all be to the glory of God!

M. Denise Baccus

CHAPTER ONE

PREPARATION FOR YOUR EXPECTATION

What Do You Expect?

For I know the thoughts that I think toward you,
saith the LORD, thoughts of peace, and not of evil,
to give you an expected end. (Jeremiah 29:11)

Prepare: To put in proper condition or readiness.[1]
Expect: To anticipate or await the occurrence of something.[2]

Always be prepared for the *unexpected*. Just how many times have you heard that statement? On the other hand, have you been asked even once, to prepare for the expected? God has given us both corporate and individual promises. Yes, primarily through His written Word but also through the preached and prophetic Word. For the great majority, if not all, in the Body of Christ, there is a deep yearning and expectation for the fulfillment of these promises; but why the delay?

Have you paused to consider that perhaps you have been in a season of preparation for your expectation? Preparation involves separation and consecration, revelation, humiliation, communication, temptation, elevation, visitation, restoration, and manifestation. In my opinion, there are very few overnight blessings. Instead, the blessings usually come when the night is over. Yes, "weeping may endure for a night, but joy cometh in the morning" (Psalm 30:5b). This process of preparation is absolutely essential if you are to come into your season of fulfillment.

Far too often, when there is not an immediate manifestation of that which is expected, believers abandon their expectations in the name of satisfaction and servitude. One such person of note was the Shunammite woman. She was an influential woman of great wealth who consistently served the Prophet Elisha. By all indications, her ministry was one of hospitality. Because of her ongoing kindness, Elisha inquired of her saying "Behold, thou hast been careful for us with all this care; what is to be done for thee?... [Her response was] I dwell among mine own people" (see 2 Kings 4:13).

In other words, she was complacent. She was financially secure, highly respected in the community, and had the comfort of her family. The popular thought that complacency and contentment are synonymous terms is flawed. To be complacent is to be completely satisfied with your present accomplishments and possessions. The complacent person is just thankful that his needs are met. Desires are simply wishes that may or may not be attained. Contentment, on the other hand, is not the abandonment of desires; rather, it is rest in the Lord, no matter what state of being we find ourselves, having full knowledge that if we:

"Delight thyself also in the LORD: and He shall give thee the desires of thine heart. Commit thy way unto the LORD; trust also in Him; and He shall bring it to pass." (Psalm 37:4-5)

"But seek ye first the kingdom of God, and His righteousness; and all these things shall be added unto you." (Matthew 6:33)

"Not that I speak in respect of want: for I have learned, in whatsoever state I am, therewith to be content." (Philippians 4:11)

YOUR SEASON IS APPROACHING

While the text does not indicate the age of the Shunnamite woman, it is known that her husband was old (see 2 Kings 4:14). We can infer then, that she, too, was past her childbearing years. When Elisha's servant Gehazi revealed the fact that she did not have a son, Elisha called for her. "And he said, '*About this season*, according to the time of life, thou shalt embrace a son.'" Initially she did not believe that she was yet capable of giving birth to that which she desired. For "she said 'Nay, my Lord, thou man of God, do not lie unto thine handmaid.'" But the prophet decreed a blessing upon her. "And the woman conceived, and bare a son *at that season* that Elisha had said unto her" (2 Kings 4:16-17, emphasis mine).

The word season indicates the time when something is at its best and in proper condition or readiness. By the mere fact you are reading this book, I believe you are closer to the realization of your promises than you can ever imagine! While the adversary has been successful in convincing some that their expectation is little more than an imagined lie, *you* recognize through faith that "all the promises of God in Him are yea, and in Him Amen, unto the glory of God by us" (2 Corinthians 1:20).

THE FAITH AND THE FAVOR

Faith determines exactly what and when we receive from God. Whereas the spirit of man is the channel through which the promise is revealed, faith is the mechanism that ensures its reality. Indeed, there are varying measures of faith. Some only possess a cognitive level of faith. While they believe intellectually that God is capable of performing mighty deeds, the idea that He will actually act on their behalf is rejected. Then, there are those who have experiential faith. These individuals find the truth of the Scripture compelling and have confidence as long as the environment is conducive to believing, but when they encounter opposition, their faith falters.

However, there are those who possess willing faith. This type of faith is a conscious act of the human will, wherein one chooses to trust God irrespective of hindrances, obstacles, or anything that challenges the Word they received from God. This faith surpasses the intellect and emotions, requiring you to grasp that which cannot be attained by human logic alone. Faith is not a passing phase; it is an ongoing attitude resulting in righteous living and full obedience "for in Him we live, and move, and have our being" (Acts 17:28). This degree of faith serves as a magnet attracting the favor of God. "For thou, LORD, [God] wilt bless the righteous; with favour wilt thou compass [surround] him as with a shield" (Psalm 5:12).

A varied meaning of the word favor is to resemble. God favors those who favor Him. How is this possible? His spiritual offspring should resemble Him in character. Just as we are drawn to those with similar personalities (often forming intimate relationships) we gain God's approval when we resemble Him in morality, thoughts, and actions. According to *Vine's Expository Dictionary of the Old*

Testament, the Hebrew word *rasôn* represents the favor that is shown in God's covenantal blessings. Thus, when Isaiah speaks of the day, year, or time of divine favor, he is actually speaking of the day when all the blessings of the covenant shall be heaped upon God's people (Isaiah 49:8).[3]

This kind of faith and favor was exemplified in the life of Mary (the mother of our Lord). Like many of us, Mary was highly favored but was baffled regarding the Lord's choice of her for such an awesome assignment. As a Jewish girl herself, no doubt she had heard about this coming redeemer, but did not readily recognize or accept God's favor. She never anticipated that she could be the recipient of such a notable blessing, for she wondered just how this could be (Luke 1:34).

Too often, God's people do not fully comprehend the fact that He has also placed a blessed seed within them. This seed, when properly nourished with faith, will grow to maturity if it is not aborted. It is common to hear the cliché "what will be, will be," even in religious circles; but let us consider the *shall* promises spoken to Mary in the first chapter of Luke. She was told: thou *shall* conceive, He *shall* be great, He *shall* reign, The Holy Ghost *shall* come upon thee, and so on. However, the angel did not depart from her until she agreed and consented to the message saying "... be it unto me according to thy word" (Luke 1:31-38).

Have you believed the promise; or is your assigned messenger still waiting for you to comply? Unlike Mary, far too many remain in the "how can this be?" stage of spiritual growth, rather than progressing to the degree of faith that says "be it unto me according to your word." Therefore, let us profess those things He has said without wavering, for He who promised is faithful (Hebrews 10:23).

5

When Mary heard that her cousin, Elizabeth, was already expecting a son, she could have easily become envious, knowing that Elizabeth's blessing would manifest before her own; however, Mary realized that this was the divine proof she needed. Now, she knew with all certainty that "there shall [would also] be a performance of those things which were told her from the Lord" (Luke 1:45).

HIDE YOUR WORDS OF PROMISE

It is interesting to note that both Elizabeth and Mary went into seclusion [hiding] upon receiving their word of promise (Luke 1:24, 39-40). In other words, they hid their words until the time of manifestation. Because Elizabeth's husband, Zacharias, did not believe the words of the promise, the angel Gabriel said unto him "And, behold, thou shalt be dumb, and not able to speak, until the day that these things shall be performed, because thou believest not my words, which shall be fulfilled in their season" (Luke 1:20). Therefore, he was rendered unable to tell anyone about the angelic encounter.

We have an additional example of when the Shunnamite woman's son of promise died, "And she went up, and laid him on the bed of the man of God, and *shut the door upon him*, and went out" (2 Kings 4:21, emphasis mine). She did not tell anyone of his death. Instead she went to the Prophet Elisha, who instructed his servant Gehazi, saying "Gird up thy loins, and take my staff in thine hand, and go thy way: if thou meet any man, *salute him not*; and if any salute thee, *answer him not* again: And when Elisha was come into the house ... he went in therefore, and shut the door upon them twain ... and the child opened his eyes" (2 Kings 4:29-35). We should also hide our words of promise from those who lack the faith to believe. Then, we too will exclaim, "The

Lord hath done what He purposed; He has accomplished His word" (Lamentations 2:17a, NASB).

As was the case of the Shunammite woman, Mary, and Elizabeth, this may seemingly be a time of barrenness in your life; but God's favor is upon you. He is going to bestow upon you everything that you expect, nothing less. Upon further examination of the preparatory process (using the book of Jeremiah as a biblical backdrop) you will clearly understand the necessary preparation for your expectation, and ascertain just how close you really are to your *expected end.*

ON A PERSONAL NOTE

Several years ago, I felt compelled to compose a written work. I immediately began the research phase, enrolled in a creative writing course, and gathered information related to publication. I began to write poetry and daily devotionals only to literally place them on a shelf in my closet. For the next seven years, I became engrossed in life and its many issues, convincing myself that I really had nothing to contribute to the literary world.

However, the suppressed desire to write resurfaced. In prayer, I asked God to tell me just what I had to offer. His response was *"You have nothing to offer me but your will. If you offer me your will, thou shalt make thy way prosperous, and then thou shalt have good success. Have not I commanded*: for *the LORD thy God is with thee thee? Be strong and of a good courage; be not afraid, neither be thou dismayed"* (see Joshua 1:8-9). With this revelation, I began to see myself as a successful author, so here I am. The promise was not null and void. I was simply in preparation for my expectation.

DEEPER DISCUSSION

Read Jeremiah 29:11. What is your godly expectation? What is your godly purpose? If you do not know your purpose, begin to pray daily that God will reveal His will for your life.

Do you feel that you have any limitations? What role does faith play?

Read 2 Kings 4:21 and Luke 1:24, 39-40. Have you hidden your words of promise? If you have revealed your promise to others, what was their response?

END NOTES

1. 1. Random House, *Webster's College Dictionary*, Sol Steinnetz, editor in chief (New York, NY: Random House Inc., 1997), s.v. "preparation."
2. Ibid., "expectation."
3. W.E. Vine, "*Vine's Complete Expository Dictionary of Old and New Testament Words,*" (Nashville, TN: Thomas Nelson Publishers, 1996), s.v. "favor."

CHAPTER TWO

SEPARATION AND CONSECRATION

Whom Do You Serve?

Before I formed you in the womb I knew and approved of
you [as My chosen instrument], and before you were born
I separated and set you apart, consecrating you;
[and] I appointed you as a prophet to the nations.
(Jeremiah 1:5, AMP)

Separate: To set apart for a special purpose.[1]
Consecrate: The submission of one's total being to God.[2]

In today's politically correct society, the biblical concept of separation and consecration has become unpopular. With the secularization of the Church and liberal institutions educating our citizens, the morally perverse spirit of Corinth has stained the moral fabric of our culture. Unfortunately, America and other nations are producing an ever increasing number of individuals who view the world and their own lives, without any regard to the fundamental tenets of the Christian faith.

While those who are separated unto Christ are criticized for being divisive and narrow-minded, the Church continues to lose its influence because the world no longer sees a difference. The once distinct line of demarcation between the Church and the "world" is now faint at best. Sadly, some no longer heed the call to holiness. Instead, they reject the truth and turn their ears to lies (2 Timothy 4:3-4). The Apostle Paul warned "that in the latter times some shall [would] depart from the faith, giving heed to seducing spirits, and doctrines of devils" (see 1 Timothy 4:1). That day is here!

RELIGIOUS INFLUENCES

As a result of our multicultural world, people are faced with diverse religions and spiritual experiences, each with its own doctrinal position. However, behind the contemporary packaging, the teachings and techniques employed by many of these belief systems can be traced back to the ancient polytheistic religions of Egypt, Babylon, and other pagan civilizations. In my opinion, there is no philosophical doctrine as pervasive or destructive to Christendom, as the New Age Movement.

The New Age philosophy is primarily based on tolerance and moral relativism, suggesting that there are no absolutes in truth or rules of conduct. Thus, proponents of this movement reject the Christian doctrine of human depravity and mankind's need for salvation, holding that all human beings share in the divine nature and are inherently good. For this reason, the atoning work of Christ is denied and the Cross of Calvary is dismissed as a fallacy. But "who is a liar but he that denieth that Jesus is the Christ?" (1 John 2:22).

Additionally, the platform of love, peace, and unity makes the New Age Movement an attractive but dangerous entity. The idea of universal oneness indicates an absence of diversity and a single moral standard. This is a direct contradiction to God's command to "be holy to Me; for I the Lord am holy; and have separated you from the peoples, that you should be Mine" (Leviticus 20:26, AMP). Remember: "Ye are a chosen generation, a royal priesthood, an holy nation, a peculiar people; that ye should show forth the praises of him who hath called you out of darkness into his marvellous light" (1 Peter 2:9). The significance of this verse is not fully apparent until you take into account divine election, the Old Testament priesthood, and the sacrificial system.

DIVINE ELECTION—THE CHOSEN OF GOD

Do you find it difficult to conform to social norms? Are you in a place of spiritual aloneness? Do you possess a godly passion that consumes your life? If your answer is "yes", it is highly likely that you are chosen of God. The biblical doctrine of election (God's choosing of one for himself) has long been a topic of debate. Whether you believe man is saved through his own free will—according to the foreknowledge of God—or by an irresistible sovereign act, is primarily subject to individual interpretation of Scripture. Therefore, it cannot be adequately discussed here. Nevertheless, one thing is certain: He chose us before the world was founded, and predestined us to be His children by Jesus Christ (Ephesians 1:4-5).

From God's choice of Abraham until now, election has always involved separation. Abraham was required to sever family ties, leave his country, and abandon his religious customs. He was separated from everything that was familiar

13

to him. This must have been painful, but remember *God never requires you to give up what is good for you.* If God has required you to abandon friendships, relocate, change employers, etc., you can be assured it is all working for your good (Romans 8:28). Israel (Abraham's seed) was also set apart by God to make them "high above all nations ... in praise, and in name, and in honour" (Deuteronomy 26:19). "And if ye be Christ's, then are ye Abraham's seed [also], and heirs according to the promise" (see Galatians 3:29). While Abraham was chosen of God, it was not his election alone that ensured the fulfillment of covenantal promises, it was also his faith and obedience.

Still, Israel assumed that they would continue to prosper and receive God's protection regardless of their disobedience. On the contrary, they were held to a higher standard of conduct and quickly punished for their iniquity because they were God's own special people. The Babylonian exile was proof of this very fact. The Lord yet chastises and corrects those that He loves so that they will ultimately produce the fruit of righteousness (Amos 3:2; Hebrews 12:6, 11).

Within the chosen nation, God further selected individuals to speak and act on His behalf. He chose kings, prophets, priests, and others. For example, the prophet Jeremiah (who was separated and consecrated to prophesy to a rebellious people) was not permitted to marry, nor have children. Thus, he lived a life of solitude, opposition, and rejection. (See Jeremiah 16:1.) While the great majority of us are not called to this degree of separation, we must be willing to give up everything that hinders the fulfillment of God's purpose. Those who do not consent are unworthy of Him. "So then, any of you who does not forsake (renounce, surrender claim to, give up, say goodbye to) all that he has cannot be My disciple" (Luke 14:33, AMP).

THE PRIESTHOOD AND THE
SACRIFICIAL SYSTEM

Israel was also called to be a kingdom of priests (offering service and sacrifice to God) but before they could minister, they were required to engage in ceremonial cleansing and dedication. Even the priestly garments were symbolic of the sacredness, moral purity, and holiness needed before one could enter the "holy place" or approach the altar of sacrifice. (See Numbers 8:5-11.) "And every one who has this hope [resting] on Him cleanses (purifies) himself just as He is pure (chaste, undefiled, guiltless)" (1 John 3:3, AMP).

The burnt offering was the highest of all offerings, partly because the entire body of the animal was consumed on the altar. Furthermore, only a clean, blemish free sacrifice was acceptable. (See Genesis 8:20; Leviticus 1:3; Deuteronomy 15:21.) As the New Covenant priesthood "Ye also, as lively stones, are built up a spiritual house, an holy priesthood to offer up spiritual sacrifices acceptable to God by Jesus Christ … [presenting] your bodies a living sacrifice,… which is your reasonable service. And [not conforming] to this world: but [being] transformed by the renewing of your mind that ye may prove what is that good, and acceptable, and perfect, will of God." (See Romans 12:1-2; 1 Peter 2:5.) Therefore, only a consecrated life, set apart for Christ, and consumed by His will, is an acceptable sacrifice to God.

For this reason, the remainder of this book is written on the foundational premise that you have accepted Christ. "For the grace of God that bringeth salvation hath appeared to all men, teaching us that denying ungodliness and worldly lusts, we should live soberly, righteously, and godly, in this present world; Looking for … the great God and our Saviour Jesus Christ; Who gave himself for us, that He might redeem us from all iniquity and purify unto himself [His own special people]" (see Titus 2:11-14).

ON A PERSONAL NOTE

I grew up in a small town in the South and was reared in a very religious home. Missing Sunday School was never an option and attending the mid-week service was an absolute must. Like many other young people, I vowed that when I reached adulthood, I would finally get to experience all that the world had to offer me.

Upon entering college, I made every effort to conform. Because I had not been very popular growing up, I decided to pledge for a sorority, only to find out that I simply did not fit in. I tried to become a part of the social scene; instead, I became more of a social misfit. The only place I really fit in was church, the one place I was trying to avoid. I soon came to realize that because my mother had dedicated me to the Lord during my infancy (praying His blessings upon my life) I was a covenant child. I could choose to be disobedient, but I would never be completely comfortable. God would always uphold His terms of the covenant to protect me, guide me, and one day make me one of His very own special people!

DEEPER DISCUSSION

What does it mean to be separated and consecrated?

Why is the New Age philosophy so attractive? What are some other doctrines that are negatively influencing the Church?

What is your view of the doctrine of election?

Is it possible to be unsaved, yet be chosen? Why or why not?

END NOTES

1. Random House *Webster's College Dictionary,* Sol Steinnetz, editor in chief (New York, NY: Random House Inc., 1997), s.v. "separate."
2. Ibid., "consecrate."

REVELATION

What Do You See?

> *The Word of the LORD came unto me, saying ... what seest
> thou? Then said the LORD unto me, thou hast well seen:
> for I will hasten my Word to perform it."*
> (Jeremiah 1:11-12)

Revelation: God's disclosure of himself and His will.

Throughout human history, man has desired to know
the infinite Creator. Because man is spiritual in essence,
there is a sincere longing to hear the inaudible, know the
unknowable, and see the invisible. While it is true that God
is incomprehensible and impossible to fully understand, it is
certainly possible to know Him in part by what He reveals
in His names, His nature, and His attributes. In theological
circles, this self-disclosure is known as revelation.

Revelation involves the idea of making known that which
has been previously hidden. The Apostle Paul wrote: "How
that by revelation he made known ... the mystery ... which

in other ages was not made known unto the sons of men, as it is now revealed unto his holy apostles and prophets by the Spirit" (Ephesians 3:3-5). It has been said that seeing is believing however, as it relates to revelation believing is seeing. Just how did Jeremiah see the spoken words of God? "Beforetime in Israel, when a man went to enquire of God, thus he spake, Come, and let us go to the seer: for he that is now called a Prophet was beforetime called a Seer"(I Samuel 9:9). This is because they were able to see both literally and figuratively.

The visible creation further substantiates the fact that it is indeed possible for spoken words to be seen. Even Jesus (the eternal Word) was revealed in a tangible way. Yes, "the Word was made flesh, and dwelt among us, and we beheld his glory, the glory as of the only begotten of the Father, full of grace and truth" (John 1:14). Therefore, if God has spoken a word about you, start expecting the visible evidence.

From the establishment of the Adamic Covenant until now, God has interacted with man in a covenantal way. Though the significance of His covenantal names has been widely discussed, it bears brief consideration. In layman's terms, a covenant is a contractual agreement between two or more parties. However, it is important to note that it is not the words of a contract that makes it legally binding; rather, it is the signature or the name that authorizes it. This is significant because *God has signed His name to every contract (covenant) He has made with you.* In biblical times, an individual's name was indicative of his total person. To defame a person's name was to literally place their character and reputation at stake.

If your character is who you truly are, then your reputation is who others think you are. God will always protect His character and reputation by defending the holiness and

WHAT DO YOU SEE?

reliability of His name. In fact, He often acts on behalf of His people simply for His name's sake (1 Samuel 12:21-22; Psalm 106:7-8; Ezra 36:20-23). Because God discloses His nature through His names and His actions, the Christian life has become somewhat experiential. This statement is not meant to argue its validity or lack thereof. Instead, it is offered because one may not fully understand the theological applications of God's names and nature, but when there is a personal divine experience, the reality of God becomes more convincing.

Shakespeare once asked, "What's in a name?" The name of God requires an inexhaustible answer. As Elohim, He is unlimited in His greatness and power. As Lord, He has all authority and supremacy. He is Jehovah-Hosenu (The Lord our maker). He is Jehovah-Tsidkenu (the Lord our righteousness). He is Jehovah-Jireh (The Lord who provides). He is Jehovah-Rapha (The Lord who heals). And the list goes on, and on, and on. However, the greatest of all His names is Immanuel—God with us. "For unto us a child [was] born, unto us a Son [was] given,... and His name [is] called Wonderful, Counsellor, the Mighty God, The Everlasting Father, [and] the Prince of Peace" (see Isaiah 9:6). Jesus is His name! (See Matthew 1:20-23.)

While the first aspect of revelation discloses who God is and what He does, the second aspect reveals who you really are, and what He requires of you. *Without a revelation of His sovereign purpose, there can be no proper course of action because there is no intended destination.* Therefore, revelation is a necessary stage of preparation for your expectation. Of course, the Bible (as God's primary revelation) should be your supreme source of truth and direction. It must remain the central component of the Christian's life and primary basis of theological convictions.

21

There are many evidences for biblical authority including the unity of Scripture, fulfilled prophecies, and the preservation of the Bible. It can only be concluded from such evidences, that Scripture is a special revelation of God, whereby He reveals himself to us. However, God has also established other means to communicate His will. This includes, but is not limited to: angelic encounters, dreams, inspiration, and prophecy. In other words, revelation occurs in ways that rational beings can perceive. This is important because revelation ceases to be revelation if there is not a rational thinking being to receive it, just as a thought cannot exist without a thinker.

DIVINE DISCLOSURE

As it relates to angelic encounters, the biblical story of Manoah and his wife (recorded in Judges chapter 13) provides a beautiful illustration. The Old Testament book of Judges provides a historical account of a righteous man (Manoah) and his barren wife. The name of Manoah's wife is not cited in the text; however, this does not diminish her greatness. Prominence does not determine God's actions toward you; rather, He responds to your faith and subsequent obedience. Even though Israel as a nation was committing evil, God sought out the righteous. *When He favors you, He will find you!*

An angel of the Lord appeared to Manoah's wife, informing her she would conceive. The Scripture does not indicate that she questioned the angel; instead, she went and told her husband. As you speak that which God has spoken, you can be assured of its reliability because [His] words will not return unto [Him] void, but [will accomplish those things He pleases, and will prosper in the thing He sends it to]. (See Isaiah 55:11.)

Manoah petitioned God for a second visitation. God honored his request; however, the angel did not appear to him. Rather, he appeared again unto his wife. While Manoah's wife did not inquire of the mystery man Manoah desired to know his name, but the angel would not disclose it to him. By His own wisdom, God has chosen not to reveal His total Being, and seldom does He reveal every particular detail of His will. To do so would eliminate the need for faith.

Perhaps, Manoah's inquiry stemmed from a common belief that if someone saw an angel or the face of God, they would die. Because of the man's glorious countenance, Manoah began to fear. "But his wife said unto him ... [God would not] have shown us all these things, nor would as at this time have told us such things as these. [As a result of her faith] "the woman bare a son, and called his name Samson" (see Judges 13: 23-24a).

Revelation can also occur through the avenue of dreams—a sequence of mental images. While common night dreams can reveal your fears, deepest emotions, and highest aspirations, they may not be of a divine origin (see Jeremiah 29:8). "For in the multitude of dreams and many words there are also vanities" (Ecclesiastes 5:7). Still, dreams have long been recognized as a form of divine communication. Consider the story of Joseph, who was both a dreamer and an interpreter of dreams.

This well-known narrative tells of the favored son of Jacob, whose dream revealed that he would someday reign over his brethren. Rather than hiding his dream, Joseph made it known to his brothers. This only further angered them, prompting them to deceive their father, and place Joseph in a pit. Remember, at times you must hide your dreams, even from those whom you trust most.

Just as Joseph's kindred were jealous of the father's favor toward him, there are those who will resent you because of the *Father's* favor upon your life. Instead of offering encouragement and prayerful support, they dig pits and devise schemes to thwart your expectation. A wise person keeps knowledge to himself (Proverbs 12:23).

Joseph's namesake, Joseph, (the husband of Mary) also received direction through dreams. He was instructed to take Mary as his wife (Matthew 1:20), escape to Egypt (Matthew 2:13-14), and to depart to Galilee (Matthew 2:22). In each case, Joseph did as he was commanded. According to The *Eerdman's Bible Dictionary*, the key to the biblical concept of obedience "involves the physical [or spiritual] hearing that [motivates] the hearer [inspiring] the hearer to act."[1] " But [for] there is a spirit in man: and the inspiration of the Almighty giveth them understanding" (see Job 32:8).

REASONING AND THE ROLE OF THE HOLY SPIRIT

"Come now, and let us reason together," saith the LORD.
(Isaiah 1:18)

Unlike animals that behave solely by instinct, human beings possess reason, intellect, self-will, and conscience. Although revelation must be viewed through the eyes of faith, reason and rationale are also necessary to distinguish truth from error, and possibility from impossibility. That being said, reasoning is based on your individual perceptions and unique experiences. For instance, two individuals viewing the same piece of abstract art, will most likely reach different conclusions as to what it depicts.

This is a result of the premise or basis upon which reasoning proceeds. Therefore, it must be said that revelation is highly personal and is subject to many interpretations. As a result, you should not expect others to see what you see. *Different destinations produce different revelations.* So how can you distinguish between true revelation and human desire? First, because God is unchangeable in His nature, history (which is truly His-story) reveals how God has acted in the past; thus, you can predict how He will act in the present. Secondly, that which is a genuine revelation tends to be the one lingering thought that remains in the forefront of your thinking. All other events then, are evaluated for their contribution toward the fulfillment of the primary thought.

Reason aided by the Holy Spirit is a key factor. His work is critical "[because] the natural man receiveth not the things of the Spirit of God: for they are foolishness unto him: neither can he know them, because they are spiritually discerned" (see 1 Corinthians 2:14). Even in times of uncertainty, "He that searchest the hearts knowest what is the mind of the Spirit, because He maketh intercession for the saints according to the will of God" (Romans 8:27).

Jesus said, "Howbeit when He, the Spirit of truth is come ... He will show you things to come" (John 16:13-14). The purposes of God cannot be realized unless you have the spiritual capacity to apprehend it. The ultimate goal should be to seize all that God has for you. "Not as though [you] had already attained ... but ... follow after, if that [you] may apprehend that for which also [you are] apprehended of Christ Jesus" (see Philippians 3:12).

THE CALL, YOUR ANSWER, NOW WHAT?

According to *Webster's College Dictionary,* the word apprehend means to take into custody, or to arrest by legal warrant or authority.[2] When you are called to a divine task, the answer should be a resounding Yes. A suitable synonym for the word call, is summon. Consider a court summons in the justice system. There are serious consequences when one fails to appear before the judge. Woe unto them who are called (summoned) by the Righteous Judge and fail to appear. Perhaps this is why the writer Paul wrote "For though I preach the gospel, I have nothing to glory of: for necessity is laid upon me; yea, woe is unto me, if I preach not the gospel! For if I do this thing willingly, I have a reward: but if against my will ... What is my reward then?" (1 Corinthians 9: 16-18).

God reveals His will to humanity because He desires to accomplish it through the human race. "For it is God who is at work in you both to will and to [work for] His good pleasure" (see Philippians 2:13). *God does not communicate His will simply to do so. Rather, He demands trust and subsequent obedience to what He reveals.* Without active obedience, revelation is of no avail. True faith always results in obedience. "Even so faith if it hath not works, is dead, being alone" (James 2:17).

Just as faith alone is inadequate, merely having knowledge of God's will is also inadequate. In fact, Adam (the progenitor of the human race) had knowledge of God's will, but his quest for additional knowledge ultimately contributed to his fall. Instead of seeking to know more, you should seek to know the omniscient One who possesses all knowledge. In the process of time, God will progressively unveil His plan.

Time (the chronological progression of events) is simply a means of preventing everything from happening all at once. Every single event that has been decreed for your life was divinely ordained in the Everlasting Covenant by the eternal Godhead. You can be assured of its fulfillment since the covenant is everlasting. Furthermore, *because an eternal God spoke the words, the words themselves are eternal. Therefore, the promise must manifest even if it seems like "it's taking an eternity".*

God's divine plan is often unveiled early in life. This is possible since we were chosen in eternity and called in time (Ephesians 1:3-5). Such was the case of the Old Covenant prophet, Jeremiah (who spoke prophetic words of divine revelation). He was reared in a godly home and was taught the Law from an early age. This was not unusual because prior to the Babylonian exile, parents assumed the major role of educators.

Much like today, Jeremiah lived in an era when standards of morality were declining and traditional values were under severe attack. Yet, he envisioned a time when godliness would be restored. There is a direct correlation between what is envisioned and what is attained. Why? What you see influences your thoughts, which in turn affects your actions, which will ultimately determine success or failure. Although Jeremiah was convinced of his own inadequacies (to the extent that he cursed the day he was born) his overwhelming determination to fulfill his prophetic call prevailed. He described it as "a burning fire shut up in his bones" (Jeremiah 20:9, 14-18).

When you have an authentic vision, it cannot be evaded. Suppressed maybe, seemingly difficult to accomplish, perhaps, but avoided, never! Jeremiah was sensitive and at times timid. In spite of his admitted shortcomings, he boldly opposed the false prophets of his time. It is important to recognize that spiritual gifts and callings are a God given grace. Therefore, the ability to accomplish divine tasks is not a result of human strength and self-sufficiency. It is rooted in Christ, who himself gave gifts unto men. (See Ephesians 4:8.)

In Jeremiah's famous letter (recorded in Jeremiah 29) he writes to Jewish captives in Babylon to oppose those who falsely prophesied that their temple would never fall. It was not the will of God that His covenant children experience failure, thus Jeremiah consoles them. He offers them hope of a return to their land, although not immediate. He prophesied that after seventy years in Babylonian captivity, God would visit them again, and perform His good word toward them. (See Jeremiah 29:10.)

His genuine call to the prophetic office made him an opponent of his contemporaries, many of whom were self-proclaimed prophets who caused Israel to go astray and walk in rebellion. In contrast, the true prophets called them to repentance and holiness. Since God is the author of the words that He conveys to the prophet, they will always be in accordance with His holy nature.

In Jeremiah 23:16-22, the writer offers the following discourse to warn against false prophets:

> Thus saith the Lord of hosts, Hearken not unto the words of the prophets that prophesy unto you: they make you vain: they speak a vision of their own heart, and not out of the mouth of the LORD. They say still unto them that despise me, The LORD hath said, Ye shall have peace; and they say unto every one that walketh after the imagination of his own heart, No evil shall come upon you.... I have not sent these prophets, yet they ran: I have not spoken to them, yet they prophesied. But if they had stood in my counsel, and had caused my people to hear my words, then

they should have turned them from their evil way and from the evil of their doings.

Although the Church continues to see an abuse of the prophetic ministry, it does not negate the value of the authentic prophetic office. Therefore "do not spurn the gifts and utterances of the prophets [do not depreciate prophetic revelations]. But test and prove all things [until you can recognize] what is good; [to that] hold fast" (1 Thessalonians 5:20-21, AMP). Prophecy, when weighed against the Scripture, and exercised under proper spiritual authority will serve to perfect the saints, equip them for work in the ministry, and build the body of Christ. (See Ephesians 4:12.)

It must be said, however, that like Jeremiah's revelation, the manifestation is usually not instantaneous; instead, you often enter a season of trials designed to promote humility and prove your total dependence upon God. "Not that we are sufficient of ourselves to think anything as of ourselves, but our sufficiency is of God" (2 Corinthians 3:5). The Apostle Paul experienced such humiliation, writing "lest I should be exalted above measure through the abundance of the revelations, there was given to me a thorn in the flesh, the messenger of Satan to buffet me" (2 Corinthians 12:7).

In the next chapter, we will examine the aspect of humiliation as the next step in your preparation. *Be forewarned, the greater the revelation, the greater the humiliation.*

ON A PERSONAL NOTE

In the early 1990s, I was called into the teaching ministry. I recall being in prayer when I saw myself standing on a blue platform speaking to a large crowd. Mind you, at this time, I was a preschool Sunday school teacher at a small church. Nevertheless, I could not get the vision "out of my head." It was my first thought of each day for the next few years.

I received several prophecies of confirmation, but for five years I did not have a single open door for ministry. I actually remember asking God to either manifest His word or lift the desire. I literally felt like I was pregnant with purpose, but lacking a spiritual birth canal. I could only hope that my dreams would not be aborted. Finally, after assuming the role of education director at a larger church, I stood on that blue platform. This was fulfilling and extremely rewarding. Except, little did I know, I would soon be humiliated beyond my wildest dreams.

DEEPER DISCUSSION

What form(s) of divine revelation have you experienced? What was your response?

Read Jeremiah Chapter 23. Have you received a word of prophecy? Do you believe that it is true? Why or why not?

What is your spiritual gift? Do you have the proper spiritual covering?

END NOTES

1. *The Eerdmans Bible Dictionary,* Allen C. Myers, editor (Grand Rapids, MI: Eerdmans Publishing Company., 1987), s.v. "obedience."
2. Random House *Webster's College Dictionary,* Sol Steinnetz, editor in chief (New York, NY: Random House Inc., 1997), s.v. "apprehend."

HUMILIATION

How Do You Feel?

They are not humbled even unto this day, neither have they feared, nor walked in my law, nor in my statutes, that I set before you and before your fathers. (Jeremiah 44:10)

Humiliate: A loss of pride, self respect or dignity, to abase, to humble.[1]

Have you ever prayed "Lord, let your perfect will be done in my life?" Well my friend, you have set yourself up for a humiliating experience. According to *Vines Expository Dictionary,* humiliation is closely connected to affliction and is often attributed directly to the purpose of God.[2] First of all, it results in your total dependence upon the Creator. Secondly, it facilitates the perfect will of God for your life.

Remember, you must "prove what is that good, and acceptable, and perfect will of God" (Romans 12:2). When good is not good enough for you, and acceptable is not in your vocabulary, the only will that is left is "perfect." Paul tells us in the very next verse how this can be accomplished. "For I say, through the grace given to me, to every man ... not to think more highly of himself than he ought to think" (Romans 12:3a). This perfection can only be achieved by abandonment of the world system, renewal of your mind, and walking in humility. In other words, as you decrease, He will increase (John 3:30).

Even though the process of humiliation is sometimes lengthy and quite painful, it often results in spiritual promotion. For "when men are cast down, then thou shalt say, there is [a] lifting up; [for] He shall save the humble person ... Thou, which hast shown me great and sore troubles, shalt quicken me again, and shalt bring me up again from the depths of the earth [and] Thou shalt increase my greatness" (see Job 22:29; Psalm 71:20-21a). *You must never lose sight of God's sovereignty when you are faced with difficult situations. Otherwise, you will focus on the pain instead of the purpose.*

Of course, God does not take delight in our hurt. Yet to accomplish His sovereign purpose, at times He allows us to suffer injustice, even at the hand of the wicked. The psalmist David was keenly aware that God allows wicked men to flourish for a time, but, "Fret not thyself because of evil doers ... for they shall soon be cut down like the grass, and wither as the green herb" (Psalm 37:1-2). God governs and controls all things, even painful events. "The Lord has made everything [to accommodate itself and contribute] to its own end and His own purpose, even the wicked [are fitted for their role] for the day of calamity and evil" (Proverbs 16:4, AMP).

This may be difficult for us to accept because we are limited by our finite thinking. For this reason, there is a natural tendency to judge God's actions by our own. This is why we must trust in the Lord and not rely on our own understanding. (See Proverbs 3:5.) This does not mean that you will never question God or even become angry. This is a natural response. Many Christians over-spiritualize that which is innate. We cannot always just "let go and let God." It is easy to make such statements to others, but how do we react when faced with similar circumstances?

Though you may be hurting, you must learn to trust God with His secrets and in His silence. Although He does not always reveal to us everything we desire to know, He has revealed all that we need to know (Deuteronomy 29:29). Yes, it may appear that your "ship" will sink, but "Now thus saith the LORD ... When thou passest through the waters, I will be with thee; and through the rivers, they shall not overflow thee" (Isaiah 43:1-2a).

History records that from the time of Israel's mass exodus out of Egypt, God continually placed His covenant people in humiliating situations to do them good at the latter end. (See Deuteronomy 8:16). Even though they were the beneficiaries of His favor, "God led [them] forty years in the wilderness, to humble [them] and to prove [them], to know what was in [their] heart, whether [they] wouldest keep His commandments, or no. And He humbled [them] . . . and suffered [them] to hunger ... that He might make [them] know that man doth not live by bread only, but by every word that proceedeth out of the mouth of the LORD doth man live" (see Deuteronomy 8:2-3).

When the Israelites found themselves in a vast wasteland, they could only imagine the worst. (See Exodus 16:2-3.) What could they possibly gain in this barren, uncultivated land? Thus, many of them wanted to return to Egypt. After all, they had become dependent upon the Egyptians and were treated with a degree of respect as long as there was a pharaoh who remembered Joseph. Even upon their exit out of bondage, they left with the wealth of the Egyptians. (See Exodus 3:21-22.)

It would only be in the wilderness that God could truly display His power and divine provision. Lest they should say "my power and the might of mine hand hath gotten me this wealth." He would cause them to know that it was He that gave them power to get wealth (Deuteronomy 8:17-18). There He clothed them, fed them, covered them with a cloud during the day to shade them, and led them by a pillar of fire at night to warm them.

Symbolically, clouds represent God's favor and manifested presence (see Exodus 40:35-38, 1 Kings 8:10-11, Isaiah 19:1), and the fire that replaced the cloud at night is indicative of a defensive covering and God's protection. (See Daniel 3:17-27.) "And the LORD will create upon every dwellingplace of mount Zion, and upon her assemblies, a cloud and smoke by day, and the shining of a flaming fire by night: for upon all the glory shall be a defence. And there shall be a tabernacle for a shadow in the daytime from the heat, and for a place of refuge, and for a covert from storm and from rain" (Isaiah 4:5-6).

From a natural perspective, clouds typically forecast an impending storm. For this reason, we are usually looking for the silver lining. Too often, this mindset affects the way Christians view life's storms. *What do you see in your clouds? I see the favor and presence of God*. Furthermore, we should not be surprised when fiery trials erupt in our lives. "But rejoice, inasmuch as ye are partakers of Christ's suffering; that, when His glory shall be revealed, ye may be glad also with exceeding joy" (1 Peter 4:13).

In the wilderness, God also revealed His commandments to govern Israel, and proclaimed His covenant blessings of land, wealth, prosperity, and an eternal inheritance. But because they did not readily heed His commandments, they would become subject to foreign rule. The Babylonian captivity was proof of this very fact. Even so, it would be for their good.

CAPTIVITY AND HUMILITY

Thus saith the LORD, the God of Israel ... so will I acknowledge them that are carried away captive of Judah, whom I have sent out of this place into the land of the Chaldeans [Babylonians] for their good. For I will set mine eyes upon them for good, and I will bring them again to this land: and I will build them, and not pull them down; And I will plant them, and not pluck them up. And I will give them an heart to know me, that I am the LORD: and they shall be my people, and I will be their God: for they shall return unto me with their whole heart. (Jeremiah 24:5-7)

How could good possibly come out of such a horrible place? After all, the very name of the founder of Babylon, Nimrod, means "to rebel."[3] But as a result of their afflictions, they would abandon idol worship, turn from the false prophets, and learn to seek God in all sincerity. Even though they were seemingly victims of injustice, *their captivity was only a blessing in disguise!* Perhaps you too can say "Before I was afflicted I went astray: but now have I kept thy word" (Psalm 119:67).

Notice, in both of these instances it was God who allowed the Israelites to be humiliated, just as it was God who sent His Son into the world to suffer the humiliation of the Cross for the good of mankind (John 3:13-17).

THE HUMILIATION OF CHRIST

"Though He were a Son, yet learned He obedience by the things which He suffered" (Hebrews 5:8).

When we speak of the humiliation of Christ, we are referring to who He was as opposed to who He became. Though He retained His deity, becoming human was an act of humiliation. As God the Son, He became Jesus the man. As the creator of all things, He became subject to His creation. As a king, He became a servant. As the heir of all things, He became our brother, making us joint heirs with Him. Though He was the Bread of Life, He became obedient to death and suffered the shame of the Cross. How humiliating!

Isaiah paints an equally vivid picture of His humiliation. He was despised, rejected, oppressed, afflicted, and a man of sorrow and grief. Yet, it pleased the Lord to bruise Him so that through Christ, His eternal purpose of redemption would be accomplished (see Isaiah 53:1-10). But for His shame, God exalted Him and gave Him a name "which is above every name: That at the name of Jesus every knee should bow, of things in heaven, and things in earth, and things under the earth; And that every tongue should confess that Jesus Christ is Lord, to the glory of God the Father" (Philippians 2:9-11). Ultimately, God will also exalt you over every enemy and cause you to be the victor. (See 1 Corinthians 15:57, 2 Corinthians 2:14.) *However, if you want to experience God's exaltation, you must first endure His humiliation.* Remember, before honor is humility. (See Proverbs 15:33, 18:12.)

HUMILITY AND LEADERSHIP

Genuine leadership always begins with the "inner man." Therefore, it is especially important for those who are in positions of leadership to have a spirit of humility. Apart from Jesus, Moses was perhaps the greatest leader who ever lived. Just maybe this was due to the fact that "the man Moses was very meek, above all the men which were upon the face of the earth" (Numbers 12:3). Unfortunately, the traditional image of leadership in the Church is that of a dictatorship with authoritative persons seeking to control and manipulate the actions of others.

This is usually a result of someone operating in the spirit of pride and arrogance, rather than humbly submitting to the Lordship of Jesus Christ (the founder and chief leader of the Church). Jesus taught against this type of leadership saying "it shall not be so among you: but whosoever will be great among you, let him be your minister; And whosoever will be chief among you, let him be your servant ... Let nothing be done through strife or vainglory; but in lowliness of mind let each esteem the other [others] better than themselves" (see Matthew 20:26-28 and Philippians 2:3).

We hear a lot about self-esteem, but very little about esteeming others. This is because we live in a self-absorbed society. Today, there are major self-help conferences focusing on self-assurance, self-gratification, self-reliance, self-worth, and the like. This focus on self has fostered the flawed idea of self-sufficiency. But the only sufficiency we have is of God, not of ourselves. (See 2 Corinthians 3:5.) However, it must be said, that confidence should not be perceived as arrogance. In fact, others do not threaten leaders who have confidence in their own abilities. For this reason, such leaders are more inclined to invest in others.

The humble leader also recognizes his dependence upon people. Even Jesus needed help carrying out His mission, choosing the "twelve" to assist Him. People make conscious decisions as it relates to whom they will follow, and will resist when they feel belittled or unappreciated. While followers are usually forgiving, they will not tolerate an arrogant leader very long and will ultimately withdraw their support. Once withdrawn, it is difficult at best for the leader to regain it.

More likely than not, Nebuchadnezzar (the king of Babylon during Judah's captivity) is not the first person you think of when we talk about humility and leadership, but his pride and subsequent humiliation provide an excellent (though extreme) example of what can happen when a leader is lifted up in pride. Daniel 4:17 tells us that Nebuchadnezzar consulted Daniel about a disturbing dream. Daniel offered the following interpretation:

> "O king ... this is the decree of the Most High, which is come upon my lord the king: That they shall drive thee from men, and thy dwelling shall be with the beasts of the field, and they shall make thee to eat grass as oxen, and they shall wet thee with the dew of heaven ... till thou know that the Most High ruleth in the kingdom of men, and giveth to whomsoever He will.".... The king spoke and said, "Is not this great Babylon, that I have built for the house of the kingdom by the might of my power, and for the honour of my majesty?" (Daniel 4:24-25, 30-31, 33)

In my opinion, Nebuchadnezzar was the literal personification of pride and arrogance. He would now endure one of the most humiliating experiences recorded in the Bible. However, in his humiliation He would come to recognize and acknowledge the supremacy of Jehovah. His own words say it best:

> And at the end of days I Nebuchadnezzar lifted up mine eyes unto heaven, and mine understanding

returned unto me, and I blessed the most High, and I praised and honoured him that liveth for ever, whose dominion is an everlasting dominion, and his kingdom is from generation to generation: And all the inhabitants of the earth are reputed as nothing ... Now I Nebuchadnezzar praise and extol and honour the King of heaven, all whose works are truth, and his ways judgment: and those that walk in pride he is able to abase. (Daniel 4:34-35, 37)

May I suggest that we all humble ourselves? *It is either humility or humiliation; the choice is ours.*

HUMILITY AND FORGIVENESS

Contrary to popular opinion, refusing to forgive others is a result of pride and self-focus. You may be thinking: "Hey, I am the one who is hurting here. What about my feelings? Why should I be the one to make amends?" Do you see the focus on self ? Yes, it costs you your pride when you grant forgiveness, and no, it does not cost the offender anything, but who ever said forgiveness is fair?

Forgiveness does not give the offender what he is entitled to; it gives him what he desperately needs. This is not to minimize the pain or excuse the offender. But when you forgive, you release the offender, making him directly accountable to God. Therefore, you do not have to take vengeance into your own hands. You can be assured; God will avenge you. (See Romans 12:17-19.) In addition, when you view the offense as an opportunity for spiritual growth and maturity, your perception of being victimized will change.

It is not uncommon for those who are called of God to endure painful experiences, often in childhood. This is because the adversary seeks to thwart the plan of God early on. Many believers have experienced rejection and various forms of abuse to the extent that the memory has become ingrained in their mind, and so deeply rooted that forgiveness seems to be impossibility. But you need only consider God's forgiveness of your transgressions. While it cost you nothing, it cost the Father His Son and cost His Son His very life. It is only when we take into account God's grace and mercy toward us that we are truly able to forgive.

It is not always easy to forgive others, especially when the offense has been especially harsh, or when we have been severely humiliated. In such instances, prayer— communication with God—is often necessary. However, forgiveness is a prerequisite to productive prayer. Therefore, "when you stand praying, forgive, if ye have aught against any: that your Father also which is in heaven may forgive you your trespasses. But if ye do not forgive, neither will your Father which is in heaven forgive your trespasses" (Mark 11:25).

In the next chapter, we will further examine communication as the next aspect of preparation for your expectation. Say what you will, humiliation, if nothing else will cause you to seek God wholeheartedly. Only then will you develop a true appreciation for your humiliation.

ON A PERSONAL NOTE

After teaching a midweek Bible study, I took my usual route home; however, as I turned into my neighborhood, I felt a weight in the pit of my stomach. It would be a few days later on Valentine's Day that I would understand why

I felt this way. After telling my husband what I desired for Valentine's Day, I received the surprise of my life. He had decided to leave. This is not to suggest that I had the perfect marriage, or that I did not contribute to its failure. Still, I loved him very much.

So like any good Christian woman, I rebuked the devil and fought for my man for the next two years. Ultimately, I filed for divorce thinking "I will show him." Just how gullible could I be? Soon after the divorce was finalized, I was forced to sell my home. I lost my car and 75 percent of the household income. I was now a statistic. I lost my husband, I lost my home, and I was quickly losing hope.

How could I teach others about the goodness and faithfulness of God when my life had been ripped apart? How humiliating! This experience really caused me to seek God. After all, whom else could I talk to? Even though my heart was shattered, somehow I had to forgive and move forward because my passion for purpose was greater than my pain!

DEEPER DISCUSSION

Have you experienced a humiliating situation? Did you question God or become angry? Did it cause you to rely solely upon God?

Did your prayer life decrease or increase as a result of being humiliated?

What "good" came out of your experience?

Have you extended forgiveness to your offenders? How did you feel after doing so?

END NOTES

1. 2. Random House *Webster's College Dictionary,* Sol Steinnetz, editor in chief (New York, NY: Random House Inc., 1997), s.v. "humiliate."

2. W.E. Vine, *Vine's Complete Expository Dictionary of Old and New Testament Words,* (Nashville, TN: Thomas Nelson Publishers, 1996) s.v. "humiliation."

3. *The Eerdmans Bible Dictionary,* Allen C. Myers, editor (Grand Rapids, MI: Eerdmans Publishing Company., 1987), s.v. "Nimrod."

CHAPTER FIVE

COMMUNICATION

What Will You Say?
What Will You Hear?

Then shall ye call upon me, and ye shall go and pray unto
me, and I will hearken unto you. And ye shall seek me, and
find me, when ye shall search for me with all your heart.
(Jeremiah 29:12-13)

Communicate: To exchange or impart information such
as facts, wishes, or thoughts. To make known. To send
messages.[1]

How often do you get distracted just when you are about
to pray? Suddenly, there is a pressing need to remove the
cobweb that has been in the corner for two months and
the phone rings for the first time in two days. I am sure
that you can relate to this scenario. Satan (the god of this
world) knows that prayer is the strongest weapon we have
in spiritual conflict. It is through prayer that our faith is
increased, and we receive the spiritual strength we need to

stand against his deceitful entrapments and cunning trickery. (See 2 Corinthians 4:4, Ephesians 6:11.)

Although our prayers are directed to the Father in heavenly places, our spiritual battles are right here on earth! Therefore, we must be diligent, persistent, and fervent in prayer.

"Praying always with all prayer and supplication in the Spirit, and watching thereunto with all perseverance and supplication.... For we wrestle not against flesh and blood, but against principalities, against powers, against the rulers of darkness of this world, against spiritual wickedness in high places." (Ephesians 6:12, 18)

In Paul's letter to the church at Colosse, Epaphras is noted for his continual fervent prayer. (See Colossians 4:12.) Here Paul describes prayer as labor—physical or mental work. Perhaps this is why the prayer life of most Christians is marginal at best. "Pray ye therefore the Lord of the harvest, that He will send forth [more] labourers into His harvest" (see Matthew 9:38). Unless we—as the harvested—become harvesters, the abundant latter-day gathering will not be realized.

WHAT IS PRAYER?

Prayer simply put, is communication between the Creator and the created; therefore, *it is the absolute highest form of dialogue.* Language (the system whereby we convey our thoughts) is one of the most important human faculties because it is the primary means by which we express our most complex ideas and emotions. Unlike the rest of the created order, mankind is endowed with the divine gift of language, speech, and voice. Because God created Adam in

His own image, his likeness inevitably included the ability to speak (a characteristic then only possessed by God and His created celestial host).

Did God equip man with this ability for the sole reason of communicating with other people? The answer is an emphatic "No!" According to the Genesis account, Adam was capable of speaking before he had another human being to communicate with. (See Genesis 2:19-20.) So is it possible that God Himself longed to hear Adam's voice and communicate with him? When we read the writings of Moses, it becomes quite evident that God does hear and speak. The book of Deuteronomy further records that the camp of Israel heard His voice out of the midst of the fire, and responded, "We have heard His voice.... We have seen this day that God doth talk with man" (Deuteronomy 5:24).

Interestingly, science has determined that we each have distinct voice patterns, pitch, and tone. Thus, your voice is as unique as your fingerprint. Just as you can easily recognize the voice of those closest to you, God also knows your voice. Like David, "Evening, and morning, and at noon, will I pray, and cry aloud: and He shall hear my voice" (Psalm 55:17). *Has He heard your voice today?*

When you truly understand the divine origin of language and the value of words, you will put away slander, profanity, and evil speaking. (See Proverbs 4:24.) "Let your speech be always with grace, seasoned with salt, that ye may know how ye ought to answer every man"(Colossians 4:6). Words are so important that even idle words will be accounted for on the Day of Judgment. (See Matthew 12:36.) Therefore, "Be not rash with your mouth, and let not thine heart be hasty to utter any thing before God: for God is in heaven, and thou upon earth: therefore let thy words be few" (Ecclesiastes 5:2-3b). Indeed, there is a time to speak and a time to listen.

LISTENING—A COMPONENT OF CONVERSATION

Listening is one characteristic of communication that is often overlooked. However, it is an essential component of prayer because it requires you to focus on the response. Prayer is not a monologue; rather, it is an interchange of thoughts and ideas. While prayer does not change the purposes of God, it can potentially change the actions of God. Your prayers can be the very mechanism that motivates God to perform those things that you have long desired.

Today He saith, "Call unto me, and I will answer thee, and shew thee, great and mighty things, which thou knowest not." (Jeremiah 33:3)

Therefore, do not fret or have any anxiety about anything, but in every circumstance and in everything by prayer and petition (definite requests), with thanksgiving, continue to make your wants known to God. (Philippians 4:6 AMP)

At the same time, we must be reminded that our Lord's model prayer opens with, "Our Father ... hallowed be thy name," not with, "I desire." Prayer, as a key component of worship, should be filled with adoration and praise. Worship refers to the "worth-ship" of God. Since He is worthy of reverence and deserving of honor, we should seek His will and His desires. As His royal subjects, we should also seek His kingdom, bearing in mind that if we seek His kingdom first, He will add everything that we need (Luke 12:31). In the final analysis, genuine prayer is never, "Let my will be done in Heaven as it is in Earth" but Lord, "Thy will be done in Earth as it is in Heaven" (Matthew 6:10).

As we further examine the aspect of communication, it is necessary to mention here, that all of the preceding aspects that we have discussed—separation and consecration, expectation, revelation, and humiliation—are absolutely essential if prayer is to be productive (abundantly fruitful). As we have learned, humiliation causes us to acknowledge our total dependence upon God and impels us to seek Him for relief of distress, if nothing else. (See Psalm 18:6 and 107:5-6.) Such was the plight of Judah during the Babylonian exile. (See Jeremiah 29:12-13.)

The prophet Daniel, who was among the captives, offers proof of this very fact in his prayer recorded in Daniel 9:1-19 for himself and his fellow countrymen. As we proceed, take note of his usage of "O," a solemn expression of pain and longing that shows the depth and sincerity of his appeal. *This is the kind of prayer that must be heard!* "For the righteous cry, and the LORD heareth, and delivereth them out of all their troubles. The LORD is nigh unto them that are of a broken heart; and saveth such as be of a contrite spirit" (Psalm 34:17-18).

Let us now briefly consider the prayer and character of Daniel, in relationship to each preceding aspect.

PRINCIPLES OF PRODUCTIVE PRAYER

1. Separation and Consecration

And it was so, that after the LORD had spoken these words unto Job, the LORD said to Eliphaz the Temanite, my wrath is kindled against thee ... for ye have not spoken of me the thing that is right, as my servant Job hath. Therefore ... offer up for yourselves a burnt offering; and my servant Job shall pray for you: for him will I accept. (Job 42:7-8)

But know that the LORD hath set apart him that is godly for himself: the LORD will hear when I call unto him. (Psalm 4:3)

For the eyes of the Lord are over the righteous, and his ears are open unto their prayers: but the face of the Lord is against them that do evil. (1 Peter 3:12)

Daniel's Prayer and Consecration

And I set my face unto the Lord God, to seek by prayer and supplications, with fasting, and sackcloth, and ashes ... I prayed unto the LORD my God, and made my confession, and said, O Lord, the great and dreadful God, keeping the covenant and mercy to them that love him, and to them that keep his commandments. (Daniel 9:3-4)

Daniel was a man of righteous character and a man of prayer, kneeling and making supplication before the Lord three times daily. (See Daniel 6:10-11.) For this reason, he was known among the inhabitants of Babylon. Even the king had heard of him. (See Daniel 5:13-14.) In fact, Ezekiel did not refer to him as a writer of Scripture or a noted prophet, but spoke of his exemplary character alongside Job and Noah. (See Ezekiel 14:14,20.) Just as Job represented his friends before God, Daniel represented his kinsmen during their servitude and captivity. His holy separation from idolatrous practices, and his spirit of excellence symbolized the divine distinction of the elect people of God, for Daniel purposed within himself that he would not be defiled. (See Daniel 1:8, 5:12, 6:3.)

2. Expectation

> Therefore I say unto you what things soever ye desire, when you pray *believe* that you receive them, and ye *shall* have them. (Mark 11:24, emphasis mine)

> God is not a man, that he should lie; neither the son of man, that he should repent: hath he said, and shall he not do it? Or hath he spoken, and shall he not make it good? (Numbers 23:19)

Daniel's Prayer and Expectation

> In the first year of his reign, I Daniel understood by books the number of the years, whereof the word of the LORD came to Jeremiah the prophet, that He would accomplish seventy years in the desolations of Jerusalem. (Daniel 9:2)

We are commanded to give careful thought and consideration to the word of God and to meditate on it day and night. (See Proverbs 4:20-22.) It is not an option. It is both our duty and our defense. (See Psalm 119:92-95 and 2 Timothy 2:15.) It is clear that the Bible should direct how we pray and what we speak. For example, Joshua was instructed not to let the book of the Law depart from his mouth and from his mind. Only then would he enjoy prosperity and success. (See Joshua 1:8.)

Daniel invoked this principle by openly acknowledging the reason for their captivity—based on the written Law of Moses—and the promised time of deliverance according to Jeremiah's writings, and he prayed accordingly. (See Jeremiah 32:42 and Daniel 9:13.) When we study the Word of God and the promises it contains, we will not be easily swayed "and carried about with every wind of doctrine" (Ephesians 4:14a). I am convinced that this is the key reason that Daniel was able to stand amidst strong opposition and persuasive tactics. He firmly believed the words of Jeremiah, who prophesied that God would bring upon them all the good that He had promised (see Jeremiah 32:42).

3. Revelation

> There was a certain man in Caesarea called Cornelius ... A devout man, and one that feared God with all his house, which gave much alms to the people, *and prayed to God always*. He saw in a vision evidently about the ninth hour of the day an angel of God coming to him ... And when he looked on him, he was afraid, and said, What is it, Lord? And He said unto him, Thy prayers and thine alms are come up for a memorial before God. (Acts 10:1-4, emphasis mine)

Daniel's Prayer and Revelation

> And while I was speaking and praying, even the man Gabriel, whom I had seen in the vision at the beginning ... informed me, and talked with me, and said ... At the beginning of thy supplications the commandment came forth, and I am come to show thee; for thou art greatly beloved: therefore understand the matter, and consider the vision. (Daniel 9:20-23)

We should never pray without the expectation of receiving divine direction and spiritual guidance. Although everyone is not called to the prophetic office, the Holy Spirit gives revelatory insight to all Spirit filled believers. "For as many as are led by the Spirit of God, they are the sons of God" (Romans 8:14).

4. Humiliation

If my people, which are called by my name, *shall humble themselves, and pray,* and seek my face, and turn from their wicked ways; then will I hear from heaven.... Now mine eyes shall be open, and mine ears attent unto the prayer that is made in this place. (2 Chronicles 7:14-15, emphasis mine)

LORD, *thou hast heard the desire of the humble:* thou wilt prepare their heart, thou wilt cause thine ear to hear. (Psalm 10:17, emphasis mine)

Daniel's Prayer and Humiliation

O my God, incline thine ear, and hear ... for we do not present our supplications before thee for our righteousnesses, but for thy great mercies. O Lord, hear; O Lord, forgive; O Lord, hearken and do; defer not, for thine own sake. (Daniel 9:18-19)

Daniel is recognized as being one of the three most righteous men in the Bible (see Ezekiel 14:14, 20), yet he acknowledged his own sin along with the sins of his people. Indeed when we come into the presence of God, we too will realize that "we are all as an unclean thing, and all our righteousnesses are as filthy rags" (Isaiah 64:6a). It is only through the righteousness of Christ and His work of atonement that we are made fit to approach a holy God. Not only is prayer to be offered in the name of the Lord Jesus (see John 14:13, 15:16, 16:23-26), it should also be offered in the same spirit of submission and obedience that characterized Him. (See Philippians 2:5-8.)

Daniel also endured severe testing prior to witnessing the fulfillment of God's promises. In the next chapter, we will discuss temptation as the next aspect of preparation for your expectation. As a precursor, let us briefly examine Daniel's temptations. (See Daniel 3:4 and 6:5.)

5. Temptation

> Then the king commanded, *and they brought Daniel, and cast him into the den of lions*. Now the king spake and said unto Daniel, "Thy God whom thou servest continually, he will deliver thee." (Daniel 6:16, emphasis mine)

Daniel's Prayer and Temptation

The familiar narrative of the lion's den should not be regarded as a fable or a mere children's story. This is a literal account of a righteous man who trusted God in the face of certain death. While few Christians today can imagine such cruel testing, all of us will experience our own degree of testing. But "The Lord knoweth how to deliver the godly out of temptations, and to reserve the unjust unto the day of judgment" (2 Peter 2:9).

ON A PERSONAL NOTE

In an effort to deal with the pain of my divorce and loss, I was called into a time of intense prayer. Initially I thought, "What is the use of praying?" *But I knew from past situations that I could always find Him on my face.* God's voice became clearer as I learned that He does not speak to the mind but to the spirit. In fact, I remember the date and time that He told me *"There will be a complete restoration of everything that you lost."* I heard it with such clarity that I immediately began to look for the manifestation.

Little did I know that *every promise is followed by a problem, and before any promise can manifest, there is a test.* I had been through enough! I had extended forgiveness, remained faithful in ministry, and now this. How could I possibly continue to believe God in the midst of overwhelming temptation? I searched the Scriptures for an answer and found solace in the familiar story and words of Job. "Though he slay me, yet will I trust him" (Job 13:15).

DEEPER DISCUSSION

Read John 10:3-5. Have you ever felt that you could not hear or recognize the voice of God? Were you still one of His sheep?

What is the role of separation and consecration as it relates to prayer?

Daniel was known for his righteous character. How do you think your acquaintances, and those in your community would describe you?

Why is it important to pray even though God already knows what you need before you ask? (See Matthew 6:8, 32; Luke 12:30.)

Today, there are two extremes evident in the Church: legalism and toleration. How can these attitudes affect one's prayer life?

END NOTES

1. Random House *Webster's College Dictionary,* Sol Steinnetz, editor in chief (New York, NY: Random House, Inc., 1997), s.v. "communication."

CHAPTER SIX

TEMPTATION

How Did I Get Myself Into This?

I the LORD search the heart, I try the reins, even to give every man according to his ways, and according to the fruit of his doings. (Jeremiah 17:10)

Tempt: To be put to the test. To prove. To examine.

THE DEBATE

Does God tempt man? Can God himself be tempted? Why did Jesus, who was both human and divine, instruct His followers to pray, "Lead us not into temptation?" Yet, He himself was led by the Spirit into the wilderness to be tempted of the devil. (See Matthew 6:13, Mark 1:12-13, Luke 4:1-2.) Why did God place the tree of the knowledge of good and evil in a central location in the Garden if He knew that Adam and Eve would be tempted by it? These are age-old questions that remain an ongoing topic of theological debate. Much of the controversy revolves around these words penned by Saint James: "Let no man say when he is tempted, I am tempted of God: for God cannot be tempted with evil, neither tempteth He any man" (James. 1:13). Still, we cannot simply disregard the numerous Scriptural passages that explicitly state—or strongly suggest—that God does tempt man, several of which are cited here:

> And it came to pass after these things, that God did tempt Abraham. (Genesis 22:1)

> Hath God assayed to go and take Him a nation by temptations, by signs, and by wonders, and by war, and by a mighty hand. (Deuteronomy 4:34)

> "God left him [Hezekiah] to try him, that He might know all that was in his heart." (see 2 Chronicles 32:31b)

> For we have not an high priest which cannot be touched with the feeling of our infirmities; but was in all points tempted like as we are, yet without sin. (Hebrews 4:15)

> "My brethren, count it all joy when ye fall into divers temptations; Knowing this that the trying of your faith worketh patience." (James 1:2-3)

THE SOLUTION

I must admit that these passages (at first glance) do seem to contradict James' assertion. So how can these apparent contradictions be reconciled? First, we must identify the grammatical context in order to determine the original thought of the author. We must also examine the "whole" of Scripture. "For precept must be upon precep ... line upon line; here a little, and there a little" (Isaiah 28:10). For example, Genesis 22:1 states that God tempted Abraham, but when we read of this same account in Hebrews 11:17, Abraham is said to have been tried.

Is it possible that it is all about semantics (the language as used in a text)? "Yes!" The word tempt is derived from the Hebrew *nâcâh* and the Greek *peirazā* meaning to test, to try, or to prove.[1] Thus, temptation (when said of God) bears the connotation of proving His word and man's faith and obedience, not seduction to evil. God's intentions are always pure and productive. *Whereas Satan is seeking those whom he may devour—fully expecting them to fall—God is seeking those whom He can promote—fully expecting them to stand* (see Ephesians 6:10-11 and 1 Peter 5:8).

Even though God permits us to encounter situations wherein our faith and obedience are tested, He remains in complete and total control. *God and Satan are not equal entities of good and evil respectively, "clashing" for universal control. Satan is a created being and is therefore subject to God's ultimate authority through Jesus Christ.* "For by him were all things created, that are in heaven, and that are in earth, visible, and invisible whether they be thrones, or dominions, or principalities, or powers; all things were created by him, and for him: And he is before all things, and by him all things consist" (Colossians1:16-17). As a result, God places limitations on our temptations and even establishes time restraints. (See Job1:6.) For "God is faithful, who will not suffer you to be tempted above that ye are able; *but will with the temptation* make a way to escape, that ye may be able to bear it" (1 Corinthians 10:13, emphasis mine).

THE PURPOSE OF BIBLICAL TESTING

As for God, His way is perfect: the word of the LORD is
tried: He is a buckler to all those that trust in Him.
(Psalm 18:30)

From the time of the first temptation in the Garden until now, promises and covenants have been subject to testing. Why? Testing is necessary because it ensures the validity of the words of the promise. For example, the marriage covenant consists of vows (solemn promises) but the truth of these words is not proven until the marriage undergoes a test. Even Jesus, the Eternal Word had to be tested and proven amidst strong opposition. Similarly, *God allows His word to be tested to prove its integrity and truthfulness.* God's word is trustworthy, unfailing, and incapable of error. Thus, His word will stand against every tactic that the enemy can conjure up. For "the grass withereth, the flower fadeth: but the word of our God shall stand forever" (Isaiah 40:8).

Not only does biblical temptation test our faith in the promises of God, it also promotes spiritual growth. Spirituality is not a religious demeanor, denominational affiliation, or a position of honor. Instead, it is the inward manifestation and outward exhibition of the spiritual fruit that Christ himself exemplified (Galatians 5:22-24). It should be noted, that every human is a spiritual being, divinely created by God. For this reason, everyone (even the unsaved) can exhibit spiritual fruit for short periods of time. Therefore, we must be willing to endure the necessary spiritual pruning to ensure that our fruit will remain. Only then will we bring eternal glory to God, and place ourselves in an ideal position to ask of Him whatever we desire, that He may give it to us (John 15: 8, 16).

HOW LONG WILL THE TESTING LAST?

Until the time that his word came: the word of the LORD tried him. (Psalm 105:19)

Psalm 105: 17-22 is a brief narrative of Joseph's stay in Egypt. As discussed in Chapter three, Joseph received a divine promise that he would be elevated to a position of rulership. However, until this promise came to pass, the word was tried, tested, and proven. Although Joseph embraced the promise wholeheartedly, others thought evil against him; he was sold into bondage, falsely accused, and all but forgotten. Still, God meant it for good. (See Genesis 50:20.)

Yes, there will be times of uncertainty, but remember God's Word will stand the test. Hold onto your promise, embrace your vision, and in the end, listen to it speak the very words that God has spoken. (See Habakkuk 2:3.) In the midst of testing:

"Just think of Him who endured from sinners such grievous opposition and bitter hostility against himself ... consider it all in comparison with your trials so that you may not grow weary or exhausted, losing heart and relaxing and fainting in your minds." (Hebrews 12:3-4 AMP)

BIBLICAL TESTING EXEMPLIFIED

But, O LORD of hosts, that triest the righteous, and seest the reins and the heart. (Jeremiah 20:12)

Throughout this book, I have utilized the writings of Jeremiah as a biblical canvas of sorts. Up to this point, we have seen Jeremiah as a candid and fearless man, who faithfully upheld his prophetic office. However, as we examine chapters 19 and 20, we gain tremendous insight into the personal life of an ordinary man who just happened to have an extraordinary calling. Here we find a distressed and bewildered man who (after delivering a prophetic decree at God's instruction) was beaten and imprisoned. Why would God intentionally send him into harm's way? The answer may be found in the following exposition:

> Then came Jeremiah from Tophet, *whither the LORD had sent him to prophesy;* and he stood in the court of the LORD'S house and said to all the people [that which the LORD had spoken].… Now Pashur … who was also chief governor … heard that Jeremiah prophesied these things. (Jeremiah 19:14; 20:1)

As a prophet to the nations, Jeremiah knew that he was called to uproot, to tear down, to build, and to plant. Therefore, it was not unusual for him to confront men of high rank (Jeremiah 1:10). However, it is quite possible (based on his reaction here) that Jeremiah did not realize that his unique calling would also expose him to extreme suffering, betrayal, and testing.

> Then Pashur smote Jeremiah the prophet, and put him in the stocks … which was by the house of the LORD.… [Then Jeremiah said] O *LORD, thou hast deceived me, and I was deceived*; Thou art stronger than I, and hast prevailed: I am in derision daily, *everyone mocketh me.* For since I spake, I cried out, I cried violence and spoil; *because the word* of the LORD *was made a reproach unto me, and a derision, daily.* Then I said, I will not make mention of Him,

nor speak any more in His name. *But His word was in mine heart as a burning fire shut up in my bones,* and I was weary with forbearing and I could not stay. (Jeremiah 20:2, 7-9)

I am certain that Jeremiah would have found it much easier to deal with the consequences of disobedience than to suffer after being obedient. But like Jeremiah, righteousness and obedience do not guarantee you a life free of trials and testing. On the contrary, they make you a prime candidate. (See Job 1:8.) In fact, Jeremiah is often called the "weeping prophet" because of the personal anguish he experienced.

Much like Job (another righteous man whom God permitted to be tested) Jeremiah has difficulty reconciling his faith with his rationale, expressing his emotions in striking similarity saying: "Cursed be the day wherein I was born: Let not the day wherein my mother bare me be blessed" (Job 3:3, Jeremiah 20:14). He even accuses God of deceiving (persuading) him to go to Tophet. Although he wants to be angry with God—telling himself that he will no longer speak of Him—he finds himself unable to do so because of the overwhelming inner unction to fulfill the word of God:

For I heard the defaming of many, fear on every side. Report, say they, and we will report it. *All my familiars watched for my halting, saying, Peradventure he will be enticed, and we shall prevail against him,* and we shall take our revenge on him. *But the LORD is with me as a mighty terrible one:* therefore my persecutors shall stumble, and they shall not prevail: they shall be greatly ashamed; for they shall not prosper: their everlasting confusion shall never be forgotten. *But, O LORD of hosts, that triest the righteous, and seest the reins and the heart,* let me see vengeance on them: for unto thee have I opened my cause. (Jeremiah 20:10-12, emphasis mine)

It is quite natural to experience feelings of anger and revenge, especially when those who know you best anticipate your demise. But "Fret not thyself because of evildoers, neither be thou envious against the workers of iniquity. For they shall soon be cut down like the grass, and wither as the green herb (Psalm 37:1-2). "Blessed is the man that endureth temptation: for when he is tried, he shall receive the crown of life, which the Lord hath promised to them that love Him" (James 1:12).

ON A PERSONAL NOTE

As expected, I experienced the usual types of temptation after being divorced. Men seemed to appear "out of nowhere" during times of extreme loneliness, and the temptation to lash out at my ex-husband was a daily battle. However, I would like to make reference to one particular test that occurred just before my separation and subsequent divorce.

While driving one Sunday morning in search of a church to visit, I was listening to a minister on the radio. I thought, "Wow, this is just the message I need to hear." As I approached a traffic light in an unfamiliar area, the minister announced the address, and I quickly realized that the church was just across the street. As I turned into the parking lot, I knew immediately that this would be my church home.

Several years later, after joining the ministry team, the pastor asked me to meet with him to discuss the youth education program. As I walked into the church, he gently placed his hand on my shoulder to direct me to his office. But it was one of the most uncomfortable feelings I had ever experienced. The meeting began innocently enough but slowly became overly personal. It ended by him scheduling a subsequent meeting, this time at a restaurant.

A "part" of me knew that he was making inappropriate advances, but "another part" of me did not want to believe it; after all, I thought he was a man of God. However, he soon removed his religious mask and revealed his true character. He began to use the most objectionable language and said the vilest things that I had ever heard from a supposed pastor. Several weeks into this ordeal, I received a phone call from my mother, who is also a prophetic intercessor. She confirmed that his intentions were not pure.

She further explained that if I yielded to his advances, my ministry would never prosper. I immediately called him and informed him that I could no longer serve in the youth education program. I concluded by telling him that I had received a prophetic warning. Of course, he tried to convince me that the prophetic warning was only a case of "mother's intuition" and should not be taken seriously.

Still, I took heed to the warning, although it was not an easy task. I remember lying on my hardwood floors, so burdened that I could barely stand. I had lost twenty pounds due to stress and depression, I was losing my husband, and now the one person I thought I could trust had betrayed me. I literally cried every day for the next full year. Why would God lead me to the one church where He knew I would experience this kind of pain? *I simply did not realize that this pain would be the price of my promotion.*

DEEPER DISCUSSION

Do you think that Pashur was used of Satan or used of God? Why or why not?

Think of a recent trial in your life. Do you think that God permitted this trial? Did you experience any spiritual growth as a result?

What methods did Jesus employ to successfully resist temptation? Are these tools available to us today?

Because of Jeremiah's passion for his life's work, he was able to stand in the midst of many trials? Why do you think so many spiritual leaders today grow weary or even completely abandon their ministerial callings?

END NOTES

1. W. E. Vine, *Vine's Complete Expository Dictionary of Old and New Testament Words*, (Nashville, TN: Thomas Nelson Publishers, 1996), s.v. "tempt."

CHAPTER SEVEN

ELEVATION

Are You Prepared?

See, I have this day set thee over nations and over the kingdoms. (Jeremiah 1:10a)

Elevate: To raise to a higher place or position. To exalt. To promote.[1]

"Congratulations, you are up for a promotion!" How exciting would it be to hear these words? Well, today God is speaking these very words to you. Unlike many professing Christians who are seeking personal enlargement apart from spiritual growth, you now possess the moral excellence and ethical standards necessary for biblical promotion. From a natural perspective, no one would expect to be elevated in rank or position without the proper skill set, or meeting the necessary prerequisites.

So it is in the spiritual realm.

For His divine power has bestowed upon us all things that [are requisite and suited] to life and godliness, through the [full, personal] knowledge of Him who called us by and to His own glory and excellence [virtue]. By means of these He has bestowed on us His precious and exceedingly great promises, so that through them you may ... become sharers [partakers] of the divine nature. (2 Peter 1:3-4 AMP)

THE SOURCE OF PROMOTION

Today, many are seeking the so-called *fame and finance* of the ministerial profession. Still others operate in a spirit of competitive jealousy. Sadly, many of these individuals are simply power-driven, attention-seekers. Of course, this is not unusual. Since the beginning of human history, there have been personal quests for positions of authority. Perhaps this pursuit stems from an innate desire to exercise power, especially when we consider the fact that man was placed in the highest position of earthly authority, and instructed to subdue and take dominion.

Unfortunately man's desire for an even higher position caused him to forfeit his earthly rule, relinquishing it to Satan, who is now the god of this world (2 Corinthians 4:4). *In seeking that which was not his—divinity—mankind lost that which was his—divine authority.* You must remember that it is God who establishes all authority, both in heaven and earth. (See Numbers 11:16-17 and Matthew 28:18.) For this reason:

Let every person be loyally subject to the governing (civil) authorities. For there is no authority except from God [by His permission, His sanction];

and those that exist do so by God's appointment. Therefore he who resists and sets himself up against the authorities resists what God has appointed and arranged [in divine order]. And those who resist will bring down judgment upon themselves [receiving the penalty due them]. Therefore, one must be subject, not only to avoid God's wrath and escape punishment, but also as a matter of principle and for the sake of conscience." (Romans 13:1-2, 5, AMP)

Thus, if you seek your own authority, you are actually walking in rebellion—opposition to authority—by pursuing a position for which you have not been authorized. Just how many people have lost jobs as a result of insubordination? How many wives have alienated their husbands by being overly authoritative or assuming headship in the home? How many children are known offenders within the juvenile justice system, as a direct result of rebelling against civil and parental authority? We must be exceptionally careful that we do not seek to promote ourselves and exercise our own authority; doing so can expose us to serious consequences.

For example, Nadab and Abihu (the sons of Aaron) were born into the priestly tribe of Levi, but they were not authorized to perform the incense service in the Most Holy Place. This was one of the highest priestly functions, and access was denied to everyone except the high priest. For this reason, they were killed immediately because they offered strange fire unto the Lord. (See Exodus 24:1-2; Leviticus 10:1-3; 16:1-2.) The NIV translates it as "unauthorized fire." *God is not obligated to accept the right thing when the wrong person does it.*

God has given each of us our very own spiritual gift, whereby we are to edify the Body of Christ. Whatever your unique path to purpose is, walk on THAT path! When you try to walk in someone else's shoes, it is very easy to stumble. But you alone have been given the grace to carry out your specific assignment, no one else. Someone is waiting to read your book, hear your testimony, patronize your business, or partner with your ministry. Are you prepared?

BIBLICAL ELEVATION EXEMPLIFIED

Let us revisit the book of Daniel. In Chapter one, we are introduced to Daniel (Belteshazzar), Hananiah (Shadrach), Mishael (Meshach), and Azariah (Abednego). While much is said of the education and elevation of Daniel, little is said of the promotion of the young men who accompanied him into Babylonian captivity. However, there are several characteristics about all of these young men that made them suitable candidates for promotion.

It is also quite interesting to note the Hebrew names of these young men. Collectively, their names bear great significance as it relates to God's role in biblical promotion. Perhaps this is part of the reason Nebuchadnezzar's commanding officer assigned them Babylonian names, and sought to teach them the literature and language of the Chaldeans. (See Daniel 1:4,7.) Certainly, this would eventually cause them to forget their own culture, religion, and even their personal identities. But as for these four children, they refused to serve the pagan gods of Babylon. (See Daniel 1:8; 3:18.) Instead, they chose to retain their identities and maintain their worship of the one true God. This decision ultimately contributed to all of them being promoted.

Daniel: God is My Judge

For promotion cometh neither from the east, nor the west, nor from the south. But God is the judge:

He putteth down one, and setteth up another. (Psalm 75:6-7)

The English word "judge" has several meanings. In the legal sense, it refers to one who hears matters, and renders decisions between two opposing parties. In another sense, it means to act as a savior by delivering someone from unjust treatment or trouble (Judges 1:2-4; I Samuel 24:15).[3]

In the face of frequent opposition, the Hebrew children were certainly in need of constant deliverance. Still, they refused to conform to the pagan practices of Babylon. They understood that God's judgments are always equitable, and are founded on the basis of His righteous law. Therefore, these youths knew that when they pleaded their case before God, the judgment would be in their favor. It may seem as if your enemies have the "upper hand" because they are in a position of power, but God is the judge. *When He renders a verdict in your favor, it is not up for debate; it is final.*

"The decision is announced by messengers, the holy ones declare the verdict, so that the living may know that the Most High is sovereign over the kingdoms of men and gives them to anyone He wishes and sets over them the lowliest of men." (Daniel 4:17, NIV)

The promotion of Daniel and his friends is a testimony to this truth.

Hannaniah—Whom God has Favored[4]

And the king spake unto Ashpenaz the master of his eunuchs, that he should bring certain of the children of Israel, and of the king's seed, and of the princes; children in whom was no blemish, *but well favoured*. (Daniel 1:3-4a, emphasis mine)

In Chapter one of this book, we briefly discussed the aspect of favor as it relates to your overall preparation. Here, we will examine favor as it relates to biblical promotion. The Hebrew *rāsôn* (favor) refers to what a king can or will do for someone he likes (Proverbs 14:35). This word also represents the position one enjoys before a superior.[5]

The Hebrew children gained Nebuchadnezzar's favor in part because they had God-given "knowledge and skill in all learning and wisdom, and Daniel had understanding in all visions and dreams" (Daniel 1:17). Indeed, "A man's gift maketh room for him, and bringeth him before great men" (Proverbs 18:16).

"Now at the end of the days that the king had said he should bring them in ... the prince of the eunuchs brought them in before Nebuchadnezzar. And the king communed with them; and among them all was found none like Daniel, Hananiah, Mishael, and Azariah: therefore stood they before the king." (Daniel 1: 18-19)

The Hebrew *rāsôn* also refers to one's desire or what one wants (Psalm 145:19).[6] In Daniel 2:48, we learn that "the king made Daniel a great man, and gave him many great gifts, and made him ruler over the whole province of Babylon, and chief of the governors over all the wise men of Babylon." God has also promised to give you favor with men. Therefore, you should not minimize the role of the people you meet, or the significance of your spiritual leaders. These are not always mere chance meetings.

ARE YOU PREPARED?

Quite often, these are divinely orchestrated encounters with successful people who will not be intimidated by your calling. Instead, they will do everything within their power to ensure that you, too, achieve success. Such was the case of the Hebrew children. For, "Then Daniel requested of the king, and he set Shadrach, Meshach, and Abednego, over the affairs of the province of Babylon" (Daniel 2:49).

Mishael—Who is comparable to God?[7]

> Blessed be the name of God for ever and ever: for wisdom and might are His: And He changeth the times and the seasons: He removeth kings, and setteth up kings: He giveth wisdom unto the wise, and knowledge to them that know understanding: He revealeth the deep and secret things: He knoweth what is in the darkness, and the light dwelleth with Him. (Daniel 2:20-22)

While God has not chosen to reveal the total sum of himself, His many names and attributes do provide us limited insight in our attempt to comprehend an incomprehensible God. The most basic name of God is Elohim. This name is always used in the plural form; however, it is not a polytheistic title. Rather, it is indicative of the fact *that all of the "god-ness" that exists is found in God alone*.

The second basic name of God is Yahweh—rendered as *Jehovah*. This name has always been regarded as His most sacred name. While its precise meaning is debated, in general it means, "I will be who I will be" or "I am who I am." This name emphasizes God's changeless self-existence. This signifies that God does not depend upon anything outside of himself for His existence and is unchangeable in His perfection, purposes, and promises. Whatever God has

77

spoken, He will surely bring to pass. (See Numbers 23:19; Isaiah 46:11.) Are you prepared to receive it?

The various attributes (perfections) of God also serve to emphasize His distinction. Attributes such as eternity, infinity, immensity, omnipresence, and omniscience belong to this classification. The attributes of God are not individual characteristics or sub-parts of His being, but each is His total being. For example, God is not just good, He is all the goodness that exists. Again, this is a difficult concept to grasp because of the incomprehensibility of God. At best, we can offer a descriptive definition of Him.

One of the most well-known definitions is found in the *Westminster Larger Catechism*. God is defined as, "A Spirit, in and of himself; infinite in being, glory, blessedness, and perfection; all sufficient, eternal, unchangeable, incomprehensible, everywhere present, almighty, knowing all things, most wise, most holy, most just, most merciful and gracious, long suffering, and abundant in goodness and truth."[8] WHO IS LIKE OUR GOD?

Azariah—Whom Jehovah Helps [9]

Shadrach, Meshach, and Abednego, answered and said to the king, *O Nebuchadnezzar, we are not careful [do not need] to answer thee in this matter. If it be so, our God whom we serve is able to deliver us.*... Then Nebuchadnezzar spake, and said, Blessed be the God of Shadrach, Meshach, and Abednego, who hath sent His angel, and delivered His servants that trusted in Him ... Therefore I make a decree, That every people, nation, and language, which speak anything amiss against the God of Shadrach, Meshach, and Abednego, shall be cut in pieces, and their houses shall be made a dunghill: *because there*

*is no other God that can deliver after this sort. Then
the king promoted Shadrach, Meshach and Abednego,
in the province of Babylon.* (Daniel 3:16-17, 28-30,
emphasis mine)

By all accounts, the Hebrew children were unyielding
in their decision to maintain true worship before God, even
in the face of death. They had absolutely no doubt that God
would deliver them, whether by life or by death. For if He
chose to deliver them from death, they would continue to
enjoy His favor on earth; but if He allowed them to die, they
would be the recipients of His eternal favor in Heaven. The
words of the Apostle Paul bear out this idea:

"According to my earnest expectation and my
hope, that in nothing I shall be ashamed, but that
with boldness, as always, so now also Christ shall be
magnified in my body, whether it be by life, or by
death. For me to live is Christ, and to die is gain."
(Philippians 1:20-21)

As the king witnessed the divine deliverance of the
Hebrew children, he simultaneously witnessed the death of
their "would be" executioners. He became so convinced of
the might of the Hebrew God, that he recanted his statements
and promoted Shadrach, Meshach, and Abednego even
higher. Whether this was due to favor or fear, we may never
know. But we do know that, "The Lord saves the godly!
He is their salvation and their refuge when trouble comes.
Because they trust in Him, He helps them and delivers them
from the plots of evil men" (Psalm 37:40, TLB).

THE RESULTS OF PROMOTION

Anointing, authority, increase, a lasting legacy, and reconciliation are just some of the results of promotion. There are many notable instances of such results, but there is perhaps none better, than those shown in the life of the patriarch Jacob.

From the time of Jacob's birth (even in the womb), he had to contend for everything that he ever received. In fact, his name was later changed to Israel, which literally means "he who strives with God."[9] He struggled with Esau to obtain the parental blessing (see Genesis 25:22-26). He contended with Laban before Rachel could become his wife (see Genesis 29:18). He also wrestled with the mysterious man prior to receiving the blessing of personal enlargement (see Genesis 32:24-26). However, these personal struggles only served to bring about his advancement. *You too will experience struggles, but each opposition is simply a stepping-stone to your next level!*

Annointing—Consecration and Divine Ability

And Jacob rose up early in the morning, and took the stone that he had put for his pillow, and set it up for a pillar, and poured oil upon the top of it…. And Jacob vowed a vow, saying, "If God will be with me, and will keep me in this way that I go, and will give me bread to eat, and raiment to put on … then shall the LORD be my God." (Genesis 28:18, 20-21)

I am the God of Beth-el, where thou anointedst the pillar, and where thou vowedst a vow unto me. (Genesis 31:13)

Not only does Jacob set apart and consecrate the pillar of stone, he also consecrates himself to God. By the mere fact that his name, Israel, yet resounds in synagogues, churches, politics, and various media outlets today, is an overwhelming testimony to the degree of anointing (consecration) in his life.

Let me be clear: anointing does not necessarily result in popularity and fame. If this were true, we would have to conclude that all well-known musicians, actors, and athletes are anointed rather than talented. Sadly, I must also add preachers to this list of personalities. Too often, good oratory skills, charm, and strong philosophical opinions are mistaken for anointing.

Promoting a man-made, self-centered agenda can be achieved through talent alone. In contrast, the anointing is absolutely essential in accomplishing a divine, God-centered task. So how can you determine if someone is anointed or just talented? The answer comes in the form of another question: Who receives the honor, accolades, and glory— God or man?

When prominent individuals constantly remind you of their status, this is a strong indication that they are self-focused, self-willed, and self-reliant. But when you are genuinely anointed, others will quickly recognize your God-given authority without one word being uttered.

Although you may never have a formal title or serve in an official capacity, when the life you lead and the impact of your words motivate others to positive change, you are truly operating in a position of authority.

Authority—Power and Influence

> Let people serve thee, and nations bow down to thee: be lord over thy brethren, and let thy mother's sons bow down to thee: cursed be every one that curseth thee, and blessed be he that blesseth thee. (Genesis 27:29)

> And Jacob was left alone; and there wrestled a man with him until the breaking of day ... And he said Thy name shall be called no more Jacob, but Israel: *for as a prince hast thou power with God and with men*, and hast prevailed. (Genesis 32: 24, 28, emphasis mine)

Notice that it was God who gave Jacob a position of power. Thus, he became one of God's delegates. A delegate is a person who is designated to act for or represent someone else. For this reason, misdirected ambition can be extremely detrimental. It is important to recognize God's ultimate authority at all times and in all cases.

Because authority is always granted, it is necessary to consult with the grantee before critical decisions are made. Acting without the proper directives is potentially grounds for demotion. On the other hand, following direct orders certainly has its advantages. Personal increase is just one such benefit.

Increase—To Abound

> Therefore God give thee of the dew of heaven, and the fatness of the earth, and plenty of corn and wine. (Genesis 27:28)

And the man [Jacob] *increased exceedingly,* and
had much cattle, and maidservants, and menservants,
and camels, and [donkeys]. (Genesis 30:43, emphasis
mine)

There is a common cliché that says, "The sky is the
limit," but when your ways please God, there is absolutely no
limit to the level of increase you can expect in your life. The
Scriptures tell us that Jacob increased exceedingly. The very
words *increase* and *exceedingly* indicate that he surpassed
others in strength, size, and greatness, going beyond any
established limits.

It is also interesting to note that Jacob's increase was
the result of a paternal blessing bestowed upon him by his
father, Isaac, (see Genesis 27) that in turn was to be passed
on to future generations. It is yet the will of God that your
children's children be blessed. You are the one whom God
has entrusted to build a lasting legacy for your lineage. (See
Psalm 103:17 and Proverbs 13:22; 17:6.) Are you prepared?

A Lasting Legacy—To Pass on to Future Generations

And God said unto him, I am God almighty: be
fruitful and multiply; a nation and a company of
nations shall be of thee, and kings shall come out of
thy loins; and the land which I gave Abraham, and
Isaac to thee I will give it, and to thy seed after thee
will I give the land. (Genesis 35:11-12)

This text clearly establishes the fact that fruitfulness
and multiplication include the propagation of offspring.
The great majority of human beings have a strong, lingering
desire to have children—yes, to guarantee the furtherance of

the human race, but also to ensure that someone will extend the family legacy.

A legacy involves more than having a memorable reputation or passing on genetic qualities. It also includes money or property handed down to another, as in the case of Jacob. The property he gained and the personal wealth he acquired were not a result of his faithfulness alone; they were passed down from his grandfather to his father, and then to him. Fortunately he possessed the wisdom and integrity to maintain them.

Today, many family legacies are destroyed simply because the recipients do not have the ability to preserve them. In other instances, when there are multiple heirs, or when one person is the sole executor or beneficiary, family arguments ensue, which only worsens the matter, as in the case of Jacob and Esau. In such circumstances, reconciliation is imperative.

Reconciliation—To Remove Enmity

And Jacob lifted up his eyes, and looked, and behold, Esau came....And Esau ran to meet him, and embraced him, and fell on his neck, and kissed him: and they wept. (Genesis 33:1a, 4)

A supposed irreconcilable difference can be one of the major obstacles delaying the full manifestation of what we expect from God. Although some Christians will not readily admit it, while they profess to be serving the God of peace, they themselves are living a life full of unresolved conflicts. However, before we can expect to experience the true abundance of blessings, we must lay aside every encumbrance that hinders our spiritual progress. (See Hebrews 12:1.)

Biblical reconciliation with others is so important that it should be done before worship and service is offered to God (Matthew 5:23-24). The Scriptures teach that, "If it be possible, as much as lieth in you, live peaceably with all men" (Romans 12:18). Jesus' earthly ministry was one of peace from start to finish. Long before His incarnation, He was given the title "Prince of Peace" (Isaiah 9:6). The theme of peace and unity was also a significant component of Jesus' Sermon on the Mount. He said: "Blessed are the peacemakers for they shall be called the children of God" (Matthew 5:9).

Notice that peace is something that must be made (produced). This means that making peace involves action. Waiting for the offender to initiate reconciliation actually hinders it. It is the responsibility of the obedient believer to set the process of reconciliation in motion. (See Genesis 32:3-6, Matthew 15:15 and Mark 11:25-26.) As long as you view another person as your adversary, you will overlook your most dangerous enemy—Satan.

Not only does reconciliation involve communication and forgiveness, it also includes consoling those who have sinned against you and reaffirming your love toward them. (See 2 Corinthians 2:6-8.) This is the degree of reconciliation that occurred between Jacob and Esau. (See Genesis 33.) As we further study the account of Jacob and Esau's reconciliation, we also learn that Jacob attempted to make restitution to Esau in the form of gifts and personal property. (See Genesis 34:10-11.)

ON A PERSONAL NOTE

After leaving the "House of Pain," I was in need of mental, spiritual, and physical restoration. Even though I was hurting, I refused to speak against my former pastor. Although I had little respect for him as an individual, I had a great deal of respect for his position of authority. For this reason, I did not take judgment into my own hands. As a result, I did not suffer the penalties of God's wrath. Instead, God placed people in my life that loved me "back to wholeness."

Within a few months, I joined another church that was led by a godly man, who imparted knowledge and understanding (Jeremiah 3:15). He also provided a spiritual covering and mentorship. Within six months I was serving as the director of the entire education program, and serving in a key leadership position. *I had been promoted!*

Today, I am reminded of these words recorded in Isaiah:

God appoints ... unto them that mourn in Zion, to give unto them beauty for ashes, the oil of joy for mourning, the garment of praise for the spirit of heaviness; that they might be called trees of righteousness, the planting of the LORD, that He might be glorified ... [And] ye shall be named the Priests of the LORD: men shall call you the Ministers of our God: ye shall eat the riches of the Gentiles ... [and] for your shame ye shall have double. (Isaiah 61:3, 6-7a)

DEEPER DISCUSSION

We have learned that God establishes all authority. What was His purpose in "raising" up Pharoah? (See Exodus 1:8ff.) King Saul? (See 1 Samuel 9:1.)

As it relates to promotion, what can be learned from the lives of the Hebrew children?

What are the consequences of self-promotion?

Why should we not take judgment into our own hands?

END NOTES

1. W. E. Vine, *Vine's Complete Expository Dictionary of Old and New Testament Words*, (Nashville, TN: Thomas Nelson Publishers, 1996), s.v. "elevate."
2. Joan Comay, *Who's Who in the Bible* (New York, NY: Wings Books, 1971), 80.
3. W.E. Vine, *Vine's Complete Expository Dictionary of Old and New Testament Words*, (Nashville, TN: Thomas Nelson Publishers, 1996), s.v. "judge."
4. Joan Comay, *Who's Who in the Bible* (New York, NY: Wings Books, 1971), 143.
5. W. E. Vine, *Vine's Complete Expository Dictionary of Old and New Testament Words*, (Nashville, TN: Thomas Nelson Publishers, 1996), s.v. "favor."
6. Ibid., "favor."
7. Joan Comay, *Who's Who in the Bible* (New York, NY: Wings Books, 1971), 259.
8. *The Westminster Confession of Faith,* Third edition (Atlanta, GA: Committee for Christian Education and Publications, 1990), 8-9.
9. Joan Comay, *Who's Who in the Bible* (New York, NY: Wings Books, 1971), 60.

CHAPTER EIGHT

RESTORATION

What Do You Possess?

They shall be carried to Babylon, and there shall they be until the day that I visit them, saith the LORD; then will I bring them up, and restore them to this place.
(Jeremiah 27:22)

Restore: To return something to its original state. To make restitution.[1]

The very idea of biblical restoration is "rooted" in Old Testament prophecy—especially in the writings of Jeremiah. Even though he foresaw the Jewish captivity in Babylon, he also predicted the restoration of his people to their own land and to their previous state of prosperity and happiness. Jeremiah also prophesied that God would make full restitution of everything that was lost during their exile.

Most certainly, many of the captives had lost all hope of restoration after such a long stay in captivity, but *where there is a living God who has pledged himself and His blessings, there can be hope—favorable and confident expectation!*

The word that came to Jeremiah from the LORD, saying ... *I will restore health unto thee, and I will heal thee of thy wounds,* saith the LORD; *because they called thee an Outcast,* saying, This is Zion, whom no man seeketh after. Thus saith the Lord; Behold, I will bring again the captivity of Jacob's tents, and *have mercy* on his dwelling places; and the city shall be builded upon her own heap, and the palace shall remain after the manner thereof. *And out of them shall proceed thanksgiving* and the voice of them that make merry: *and I will multiply them,* and they shall not be few; *I will also glorify them,* and they shall not be small. (Jeremiah 30:1, 17-19, emphasis mine)

Moreover the word of the LORD came unto Jeremiah the second time, while he was yet shut up in the court of the prison, saying ... I will cause the captivity of Judah and the captivity of Israel to return, and will build them, as at the first ... *And it shall be to me a name of joy, a praise and an honour before all the nations of the earth, which shall hear all the good that I do unto them: and they shall fear and tremble for all the goodness and for all the prosperity that I procure unto it.* (Jeremiah 33:1,7,9, emphasis mine)

Even though the nation of Israel was seen as a cultural and religious outcast, God was committed to His covenantal promise to bless them. We all have experienced rejection to some degree, and at times have felt as though God has forgotten His promises. *But God does not forget and He does not reject; He fully restores!* As we can see from the passages cited above, restoration includes goodness and mercy, glory and honor, healing, multiplication, and praise and thanksgiving. Let us examine each of these components of restoration:

GOODNESS AND MERCY

O give thanks unto the LORD, for he is good: for his mercy endureth for ever. (Psalm 107:1)

The English word goodness indicates kindness, generosity, favor, and well-being. The Greek *chrēstotēs* signifies that goodness is not merely a quality, but it is also an action.[2] For this reason, goodness must have a source and a recipient. For example, no one can deem you to be a good person, apart from the demonstration of good actions. As it relates to God, the very essence of His character is good. Thus, we can conclude that His actions toward us must also be good.

In the Book of Beginnings, Genesis, we are introduced to an eternal God, who spoke light and life into a world of vast emptiness and darkness. Genesis Chapter one records that everything God spoke into creation was called good. In other words, God took something that was formless and chaotic, and created something that was useable, orderly, and gloriously good! God will also take that which you have determined to be bad, and cause it to produce something good (Romans 8:28). You must remember that God's goodness is most apparent when it can be contrasted with evil; and His glorious light can only be revealed in darkness.

From a biblical perspective, goodness manifests itself both spiritually and materially. This truth is no more evident than in the words of Jehovah himself recorded in Exodus 3:7-8, 21 wherein:

> The LORD said, "I have surely seen the affliction of my people ... and have heard their cry ... *I know their sorrows; and I am come down to deliver them out of the hand of the Egyptians, and to bring them up*

91

out of that land unto a good land ...flowing with milk and honey.... And I will give this people favour in the sight of the Egyptians: and it shall come to pass, that, when ye go, ye shall not go empty [handed]."

In this passage, not only do we see the goodness of the Lord, but we also see His mercy. Mercy may be defined as compassion to one in distress. It can also denote the favor of a superior to an inferior.[3] Just as God is the source of all goodness, He is also the "Father of Mercies" (2 Corinthians 1:3). This combination of goodness and mercy is found throughout the Scriptures, and they are virtually inseparable. (See 1 Chronicles 16:34, Ezra 3:11, and Psalm 106:1.) It is interesting to note that both of these actions are acts of God, and require no effort on the part of the recipient. Thus, God alone receives the praise, the glory, and the honor.

Perhaps these popular words of the Psalmist David illustrate it best:

> *"The LORD is my shepherd* [to feed, guide, and shield me]; I shall not lack ... *He* refreshes and restores my life (my self); *He* leads me in the paths of righteousness [uprightness and right standing with Him—not for my earning it, *but] for His name' sake....* Surely or only goodness, mercy, and unfailing love shall follow me all the days of my life, and through the length of days the house of the Lord [and *His* presence] shall be my dwelling place." (Psalm 23:1,3-4, 6, AMP, emphasis mine)

GLORY AND HONOR

But glory, honour, and peace, [is given] to every man that worketh good. (Romans 2:10)

The word glory is often rendered as honor. It denotes those characteristics in an individual that are worthy of respect and admiration. This is not to be misunderstood as worship (which belongs solely to God). Rather, it conveys the idea that mankind is crowned with glory as the pinnacle of God's creation and was divinely created to be a vessel of honor, suitable for His use. (See Psalm 8:5, 2 Timothy 2:21.) God accomplished this by endowing man with various aspects of himself, making us objects of honor in which He could take pride.

The Hebrew word *kābôd,* meaning glory, bears an even stronger emphasis. It refers to a great quantity, rank, and distinction.[4] Because we were created for the purpose of reflecting the character and image of God in the Earth, this inevitably includes might, majesty, ruler-ship, wealth, and wisdom. Of course, "Wisdom is the principal thing; therefore get wisdom: and with all thy getting get understanding. Exalt her, and she shall promote thee: She shall bring thee to honour, when thou dost embrace her. She shall give to thine head an ornament of grace: a crown of glory shall she deliver to thee" (Proverbs 4:7-9).

Having patiently completed each stage of preparation, your focus has now shifted to kingdom building and the advancement of your godly purpose. Like King Solomon, you have not asked for wealth and recognition, rather you have asked for spiritual things. It is for this very reason that you can be trusted with the abundance of His blessings and are prepared to "handle" the favor that is about to overtake you. Today, God says to you "Because thou hast asked

93

[for spiritual things], behold I have given thee a wise and understanding heart.... And I have also given that which thou hast not asked, both riches and honour" (see 1 Kings 3:11-13a).

HEALING

I have seen his ways, and will heal him: I will lead him also, and restore comforts unto him and to his mourners.
(Isaiah 57:18)

Undoubtedly, those who had been in exile were deeply wounded. After all, they had been displaced from their homeland, robbed of their religious freedoms, and subjected to foreign domination. For this reason, we can conclude that many of them were suffering from depression, despair, and were likely in a state of desperation. All of which has been scientifically linked to various physical illnesses.

Fortunately, Israel had a covenantal promise of healing from Jehovah-Rapha, the God who heals *all* diseases (see Psalm 103:3). To be healed means to be restored to full health, both physically and spiritually. In fact, God was so committed to their complete healing, that He spoke against the false prophets of that day, who only offered temporary and symptomatic relief, saying, "They have healed also the hurt of the daughter of my people *slightly* saying, peace, peace, when there is no peace" (Jeremiah 6:14; 8:11, emphasis mine). *God never partially heals us,* whether it is through divine or medical intervention.

In the Old Testament, divine healing was primarily a result of faith and obedience. (See Exodus 15:26.) However, various medicines were also used including oil, wine, myrhh, and various plants. For example, in Jeremiah's writings, he sometimes refers to the balm of Gilead—an aromatic healing salve, derived from a common plant (see Jeremiah 8:22, 46:11). Gilead itself was also a "city of refuge" which provided a place of protection from danger (see Genesis 31:21, 1 Samuel 13:7). But there is also a "sovereign" balm of Gilead that is able to heal our deepest and most severe wounds, and provide safety in the time of trouble. It is found in the Good Physician, Jesus Christ, who was wounded so that we could be healed.

> *"Surely, He hath borne our griefs, and carried our sorrows ...* He was wounded for our transgressions [and] he was bruised for our iniquities: the chastisement of our peace was upon him; and *with his stripes we are healed."* (Isaiah 53:4-5, emphasis mine)

MULTIPLICATION

And he will love thee, and bless thee, and multiply thee: he will also bless the fruit of thy womb, and the fruit of thy land ... Thou shalt be blessed above all people. (Deuteronomy 7:13-14a)

Multiplication means an increase in number or greatness. This word also denotes an overwhelming abundance and unprecedented growth.[5] Consider God's first command to mankind "be fruitful and multiply" (Genesis 1:22). Notice, that God did not give Adam and Eve this command until after He blessed them. Secondly, He placed them in an environment that was suitable for growth and increase.

> *And a river went out to Eden to water the garden;* and from thence it was parted ... The name of the first is Pison: that is it which compasseth the whole

land of Havilah, *where there is gold; And the gold of that land is good; and there is [aromatic resin] and the onyx stone*. (Genesis 2:10-12, emphasis mine)

It was only when Adam and Eve stepped out of divine positioning that they were required to labor in order to receive a harvest. However, as part of the restorative process, God has repositioned you for fruitfulness and multiplicity. I believe that He is about to take you from a spiritual desert to a place of abundance. Yes, you went through fire and through water, but now He is bringing you into a wealthy place (see Psalm 66:12).

When Abraham was repositioned, God blessed him and multiplied his goods. He also promised to increase and multiply his seed as a continuance of the covenant He made with him (see Gen 12:1-3). "For when God made promise to Abraham, because He could sware by no greater, He sware by Himself saying surely blessing I will bless thee, and multiplying I will multiply the" (Hebrews 6:13-15). "And if ye be Christ's, then are ye Abraham's seed, and heirs according to the promise" (Galatians 3:29).

PRAISE AND THANKSGIVING

Oh that men would praise the LORD for his goodness, and for his wonderful works to the children of men.
(Psalm 107:8)

Praise is the joyful expression of admiration to God. While praise is directed toward God for who He is, thanksgiving is offered as a result of what He does. Of course, our praise should not be predicated upon our circumstances, but if we are truly honest, we will acknowledge that personal trials, difficulties, and the like can quickly diminish our "joy level."

On the other hand, when we experience the goodness of God and witness His mighty acts, our praise and thanksgiving is immediately restored. For example, when the children of Israel witnessed the defeat of the Egyptian army, they exited out of bondage with praise.

> Then sang Moses and the children of Israel this song unto the LORD, and spake, saying, I will sing unto the LORD, for he hath triumphed gloriously.... The LORD is my strength and song, and he is become my salvation: he is my God, and I will prepare him an habitation; my father's God, and I will exalt him ... And Miriam the prophetess, the sister of Aaron, took a timbrel in her hand; and all the women went out after her with timbrels and with dances. (Exodus 15:1-2, 20)

As a result of this glorious triumph, they went from prison to praise, and from sadness to singing. May this be your testimony!

ON A PERSONAL NOTE

As a result of being promoted, I was literally thrust "into the spotlight" so to speak. My life became anopen book read of men (2 Corinthians 3:2). Unbeknownst to me, God had placed me in a position where others would not only hear my testimony, but also witness my restoration. Just as creation declares the goodness and riches of God to all who behold it (see Psalm 33:5; 104:24), I believe that God also desires to make you a recipient and public example of what it truly means to be blessed!

Perhaps, like me, you are in the very heart of the restorative process, but I am convinced that the best is yet to come—and quickly. In the brief interim, let us hold fast to these words recorded in Joel 2:25-26:

> I will restore to you the years that the locust hath eaten, the cankerworm, and the caterpillar, and the palmerworm.... And ye shall eat in plenty, and be satisfied, and praise the name of the LORD your God, that hath dealt wondrously with you: and [you] shall never be ashamed.

DEEPER DISCUSSION

Loss is a necessary prerequisite to restoration. Why do you think that God would permit loss in your life?

Read Jeremiah 33:1-9. In what ways has the goodness of God been revealed in your life? Is it apparent to others?

Mercy basically means "compassion." Why do you think mercy often accompanies goodness in the Scriptures?

Do you think that "increase" is a necessary component of restoration, or an added benefit? Why or why not?

END NOTES

1. Random House *Webster's College Dictionary*, Sol Steinnetz, editor in chief (New York: NY: Random House, Inc., 1997), s.v. "restoration."
2. W.E. Vine, *Vine's Complete Expository Dictionary of Old and New Testament Words*, (Nashville, TN: Thomas Nelson Publishers, 1996) s.v. "goodness."
3. Ibid., "mercy."
4. Ibid., "glory."
5. Random House *Webster's College Dictionary*, Sol Steinnetz, editor in chief (New York: NY: Random House, Inc., 1997), s.v. "multiply."

✿

CHAPTER NINE

MANIFESTATION

The Wait Is Over!

Behold, the days come, saith the LORD, that I will perform that good thing which I have promised. (Jeremiah 33:14)

Manifestation: Readily perceived by the eye, evident, to make clear.[1]

Inevitably, there is always an interval of time between the promise and the performance; otherwise, there would be no need for a promise. But I have good news. The wait is finally over, and there is about to be a manifestation of your expectation! When we consider the word manifestation, it must be evaluated on the basis of what we have been promised, and more importantly, who made the promise. This is extremely important because the promise is no more reliable than the source.

For example, has anyone ever promised you that they would meet you for lunch at twelve o'clock, only to find themselves furiously searching for their keys at one-thirty? Or has someone given their word that they would complete an assigned task, just to drop the ball when they realized the amount of work involved?

Of course these are simple illustrations, but they serve to justify the fact that we, as members of the human family, sometimes break promises. This is not to suggest that we do so intentionally; but the bottom line is that we all have made promises that for one reason or another we did not keep. Many times this is simply due to unforeseen circumstances. But unlike men, God knows the future perfectly; therefore, He is always reliable, unchangeable, and never breaks a promise. (See James 1:17.)

THE PROMISES OF GOD

For all the promises of God in him are yea, and in him Amen. (2 Corinthians 1:20)

In contrast to the promises of men, which may or may not be fulfilled, the promises of God are unfailing and true because they are in Him. Thus, there can be no greater security. Even God made an oath by himself. "For when God made promise to Abraham, because he could swear by no greater, he sware by himself" (Hebrews 6:13). In Scripture, not only does faithfulness apply to God, but it also applies to His word (see 1 Thessalonians 5:24, Titus 1:9). This means that the Word of God is just as reliable as He himself. This provides us two-fold assurance that His Word will indeed come to fruition.

Similarly, the promises of God are "Yea" and "Amen." This double affirmation further emphasizes the reliability of God's promises. *Yea* indicates that something has been confirmed to be true.[2] *Amen* literally means, "It is so and shall be so."[3] Simply put, *yea* confirms the truth of God's word, and *amen* serves as a witness to its truth. This was ultimately revealed in Jesus Christ (see John 1:1, 14-17), who is the Truth (see John 14:6) and "the Amen, the faithful and true witness" (Revelation 3:14). For this reason, whatever you ask of the Father in the name of Jesus will be given to you (see John 14:13-14). Expect it now!

THE TIME OF THE PROMISE

To every thing there is a season, and a time to every purpose under the heaven:... He [God] hath made every thing beautiful in his [its] time:... whatsoever God doeth, it shall be for ever: nothing can be put to it, nor anything taken from it: and God doeth it, that men should fear [revere and worship] before Him.
(Ecclesiastes 3:1, 11a, 14)

We only need to consider the cycles of nature, and the seasons of the year to clearly see the wisdom of God (Psalm 136:5), and appreciate His impeccable timing. Everything in creation is so perfectly planned, and divinely orchestrated that it is truly awe inspiring. You can take comfort in knowing that the plans of God (once set in motion) cannot be altered. The sun and moon yet govern the skies, and the earth continues to rotate on its axis. "While the earth remaineth, seedtime and harvest, and cold and heat, and summer and winter, and day and night shall not cease" (Genesis 8:22).

Just as God placed the towering oak inside of an acorn, and untold beauty in the seed of a flower, He also placed great potential inside of you, and ordained spiritual seasons for your life. Yes, you endured the harsh barren winter season, and the dry summer season, and today you have reached the season of blessings. Now is the time of the promise!

THE PROMISE FULFILLED

Now in the first year of Cyrus king of Persia, that the word
of the LORD by the mouth of Jeremiah might be fulfilled,
the LORD stirred up the spirit of Cyrus [so] that he made
a proclamation throughout all his kingdom, and put it also
in writing, saying, Thus saith Cyrus king of Persia, The
LORD God of heaven hath given me all the kingdoms of
the earth; and he hath charged me to build him an house
at Jerusalem, which is in Judah. Who is there among you
of all his people?... Let him go up to Jerusalem, which
is in Judah, and build the house of the LORD God of
Israel ... And whosoever remaineth in any place where he
sojourneth, let the men of his place help him with silver,
and with gold, and with goods, and with beasts, beside the
freewill offering for the house of God that is in Jerusalem.
Also Cyrus the king brought forth the vessels of the house
of the LORD which Nebuchadnezzar brought forth out of
Jerusalem. (Ezra 1:1-4)

As we revisit our text story, we reach the fulfillment of Jeremiah's prophecy. As the Book of Ezra opens, the writer introduces us to a new king, Cyrus, whom God raised up for the purpose of accomplishing His word, as spoken by Jeremiah. (See Isaiah 44:24-28, 45:1-3.) While the Scriptures do not indicate that Cyrus worshipped the God of the Jews, it is very apparent that the Spirit of God influenced him. Yes, earthly rulers have a limited degree of power, but the plans of God are not accomplished by the might or power of men, but by the Spirit of the Lord. (See Deuteronomy 8:15-17, Zechariah 4:6.)

In Jewish history, Cyrus is remembered as a generous and sympathetic ruler because he granted them permission to return to Jerusalem and rebuild the Temple. This proclamation of freedom was put in writing and published throughout Cyrus' vast empire. Remember, God desires to make you a public example of what it means to be divinely blessed. Not only did Cyrus proclaim the freedom of the Jews, but he also made arrangements for others to assist them with finances and material goods, and ordered that the Temple vessels be restored.

It is interesting to note that these vessels were to be used in worship to God. Worship is the very thing that God desired of His people from the founding of their nation, even until now. Maybe, just maybe, God has brought us through all of this simply because He desires our worship. Selah.

ON A PERSONAL NOTE

Well, here I am. The wait is over! At this very moment I am writing the concluding sentences to my first inspirational book, and I must admit that it feels fantastic! Even though the completion of this book is the fulfillment of a personal divine promise, I pray that it has also served to confirm that the manifestation of your expectation is "at hand." If I have never been certain of anything, I am absolutely "... confident of this very thing, that he which hath begun a good work in you will perform it until the day of Jesus Christ" (Philippians 1:6).

May the grace of God be with you all, yea and amen!

DEEPER DISCUSSION

Man often changes his plans for various reasons. What day-to-day factors contribute to our failure in keeping promises?

The Scriptures clearly teach that both God and His word are faithful. In what ways has God demonstrated this truth in your life?

All promises have a purpose. What is the purpose of your divine promise? Is the overall purpose solely for your benefit, or is it also for the benefit of others?

END NOTES

1. Random House *Webster's College Dictionary*, Sol Steinnetz, editor in chief (New York: NY: Random House, Inc., 1997), s.v. "manifestation."
2. W.E. Vine, *Vine's Complete Expository Dictionary of Old and New Testament Words*, (Nashville, TN: Thomas Nelson Publishers, 1996) s.v. "yea."
3. Ibid., "amen."